How Knowing Your Identity Lets You Live Your True Purpose

ARE YOU WHO YOU WANT TO BE

DAMIAN GERKE

Advance Praise for
Are You Who You Want to Be and Field Guide

"Damian offers **a state of the union on the world's perilous and insatiable search for identity, and the alternative path for followers of Jesus.** An increased competency in identity formation is critical for missional leaders in contemporary society, and this book is a great place to start."

Lucas Pulley
Executive Director, Underground Network, Tampa, FL

"I have such respect for Damian Gerke. His life and leadership inspire me. As I work with young professionals, one of the core issues that each seems to face is that of living out of their true purpose. We can spend countless years searching for the wrong purpose, yet **what if we truly lived out of our identity? If you are searching for how to find your identity and purpose, this book is for you.** No matter your background in faith, Damian does a fabulous job unpacking the truth of identity through the lens of Jesus."

Jason Soderstrom
Lead Pastor, Restoration Church, Denver, CO
Founder of The Brook, a Denver-based global movement of young, professional, everyday disciples making disciples for generations to come

"Our culture today sees a failing and collapsing social construct within the next generation. In the book and Field Guide, *Are You Who You Want to Be*, the author grounds the reader with the most important questions being asked today within rising Generations Z and Alpha: Who am I? And what is my identity? The book **builds the social construct for the reader to understand the importance of authenticity, transparency, and transformational identity.** The book **drives the thoughts that there will never be another you.** You are custom-made by God and for God, so live within your uniqueness from God."

Dr. Gary J. Moritz
Lead Pastor, City United Church, Lunenburg, MA
Revitalization and Renewal SME and Associate Professor, Liberty University
Director of Revitalization and Renewal, Baptist Churches of New England
President, The Church Vitality Network

"**Finally, here's a book that answers a question that all humanity desperately struggles with: 'Who am I, and what is my purpose for living?'** I deal with veterans who wrestle with these questions on a daily basis. For them—and for us all—identity and purpose are paradoxes: Obscure, vague concepts that are also intimate, personal and existentially vital. *Are You Who You Want to Be* **resolves the paradoxes of identity and purpose in a way that is both comprehensible and practical.** The stories Damian uses to draw out the principles of identity formation are relatable and human. They draw me in: I can see myself and my own identity journey as I read through these pages. This book **invites you to wonder, 'How am I part of God's story—and how is he a part of mine?'** I'm excited to see this book in the hands of military members, veterans and their families—it will be a game changer!"

Kevin Weaver, Director, The Warrior's Journey

"We live in a time where anxiety and depression in the next generation are at an all-time high. Without a doubt, the statistics reveal that **we are at the peak of a mental health crisis.** Many dynamics play into this crisis, but one of the primary reasons is identity crisis. **We are facing an unprecedented identity crisis in a generation.** Who am I? What determines my identity? What is the purpose of life? Damian's ***Are You Who You Want to Be* (the book and *Field Guide*) is the right resource for this moment in time**, bringing clarity to these questions with a depth of insight, practical wisdom, and compelling prose. **You will want to share this with everyone whom you care about**."

Rob Wegner, Founder, Kansas City Underground, Kansas City, MO;
Co-author of *The Starfish and The Spirit*
North American Director, NewThing Network
Director of Microchurch NEXT, Leadership Network

"**Life is about a Who, not a what; who we are becoming more than what we're doing, Who we do it for more than what we do it for.** Identity is the gearbox for the engine of everybody's life, and for most, it's disengaged, causing frustration and disappointment. Gerke **offers a journey towards liberation and the adventure of purpose everyone yearns for**."

Mike Sharrow, CEO, C12 Business Forums

"We can spend much of our lives trying to forge an identity "from the outside in." We let our careers, our families, our possessions, and our pursuits define us. In *Are You Who You Want to Be*, Damian Gerke **describes a better way to the true identity you were born to know—the one God gave you.**"

Bill Couchenour, Director of Deployment, Exponential

"In a world where people struggle to find a rudder for their lives, Damian provides a road map to God's purpose for their lives. He helps them find themselves through his storytelling and guides them to the path of life. This is a great tool to help someone find purpose."

Dr. Jomo Cousins, Lead Pastor of Love First Christian Center
Former NFL player, motivational speaker, radio host
and author of *How to Hear God* and *The ABCs' of Success*

This book by Damian Gerke, *Are You Who You Want to Be*, **could not have come into existence at a more divinely appointed time**. It is a marvelous and definitive contribution to society's confused narratives addressing the identity crisis that is ripping families, genders and self-identities into competing and fragmented pieces. **Damian's gentle and calming voice provides a proven alternative to the world's chaotic screams** that tear at the very foundational seams holding our social structures together.

Damian's soothing and wisdom-based approach **goes to the very heart of one of the world's oldest and most haunting questions: "Who Am I?"** He frames his theologically-sound guidance on proven and reliable counsel from God's Word. In a step-by-step and easy-to-follow manner, the reader can confidently come to answers to nagging queries that may have been swirling in their minds for years. **People reading and applying his advice will be set free from personal self-doubts** and can silence the world's misinformation in this vital area that will enable a person to experience the peace that passes all understanding.

LaVon Koerner, Executive Director, Christian Business Fellowship
Entrepreneur, minister and author of *Navigating the Seven Desires of your Heart* and *Life's Joy Killers and Joy Makers*

Publish@nowscpress.com
www.PublishWithNOW.com
@nowscpress

Ordering Information:

Quantity sales. Special discounts are available on quantity purchases by corporations, associations, and others. For details, contact the publisher at the address above.

Orders by U.S. trade bookstores and wholesalers. Please contact: NOW SC Press: Tel: (813) 970-8470 or visit www.PublishWithNOW.com

Bible Scriptures generally are taken from the NEW INTERNATIONAL VERSION (NIV) unless otherwise indicated

Printed in the United States of America

First Printing 2023

ISBN: 979-8-9870349-7-2

DEDICATION

To Suzie:
Thank you for the courage you display
in becoming a small and beautiful version of Jesus
no one has ever seen before.

Contents

PART 3
Altering Life's Rhythms

PART 4
So … Now What?

PART 5
Putting It Into Perspective

Introduction

Who am I?

Have you asked yourself that question recently?

The usual answers include our names, where we live, or what we do for work or fun. These are great and appropriate for the *so-tell-me-about-yourself* question we hear when we meet someone for the first time.

But they're insufficient in ways we can't fully explain. They're superficial, like placeholders for something more profound. They're not who we are *really*—at the deepest level, where we can be known as unique beings.

"Who am I?" is both an inviting and haunting question, one we've probably asked ourselves all our lives. It's a dilemma, this question of identity. On the one hand, we desperately long to know who we are. But on the other hand, we don't even know what we're looking for, much less how to find it.

And so, our true identity remains elusively and tauntingly just beyond reach.

Am I who I want to be?

It's like asking, "Who am I?" except it's more purposeful. It has an aspirational tone, hinting at an ideal identity waiting to be discovered. It reveals a gap between who we are now and who we want to be, or who we think we could be—or should be.

That gap—and the effort and attention we give toward closing it—is why I wrote this book. The gap defines a longing you may or may not be aware of. It's part of the human condition, common to all of us and unique to each of us.

My answer to the *so-tell-me-about-yourself* question is that I'm an author and leadership coach. I write about stuff to help make sense of things I'm passionate about. I've been coaching people in the areas of leadership, development, business, church strategy, and spiritual formation for 15 years. Before that, I was a vocational minister for another 15 years, after a decade of working as an engineer in the aerospace industry.

I've been a sounding board for hundreds of people during thousands of hours of pastoral and coaching conversations, walking through their highest highs and lowest lows. In these safe and vulnerable conversations, they always came away with new, fresh and healthy perspectives by discussing who they were and who they wanted to be.

Those conversations revealed a couple of interesting patterns. First, "Are you who you want to be?" was a big question. Typically, there was often a long pause followed by, "That's a good question." Many had never considered it. Many others didn't want to answer it—as if it was too lofty or as if answering it might jinx them.

The second pattern is that people usually identify themselves by their activities, achievements and relationships. These are easy to measure, and their impact on shaping us is obvious. But what's less obvious is how much we over-rely on them to define us. It's almost as if we don't have any other way to describe who we are and who we want to be.

Or so we think.

I wrote this book for those who are searching, looking for that thing they can't quite get their minds around. It's for those who believe that there's more to being human than can be seen, felt and touched; more than what we do, build or create. And certainly, more than what people say about us.

My goal is to unveil a better way to think about who we are and a practical way to become who we want to be. And in knowing who we want to be, we can have an awareness of how to engage in this life and fulfill our unique purpose, individually and collectively.

To do this, I'll be using stories, some from my life and some from other people. I tried writing about identity in technical terms, but it was too abstract. Plus, it was boring. So, I'm using stories instead.

Stories are powerful, memorable and relatable. Stories have morals that are more caught than taught. They create more questions than answers. I like answers. They're convenient and easy. But looking back, I've always learned more by asking questions than by getting answers.

I'll be asking lots of questions.

Each chapter is a collection of separate "scenes" that contrast and complement one another to make a point. They might be hard to follow at the beginning, like one early reviewer who said, "The manuscript kinda jumps around." I encourage you to wait for all the scenes to fall into place as you read since they may not make sense at first.

That's the story of life anyway. It's rarely revealed as a whole, sequentially and in an upfront way. It comes at us in vignettes that don't immediately sync. The mosaic of life's experiences is always *coming* together.

Hopefully, the *Disambiguation Section* at the end of each chapter that summarizes the main points will help reduce the "jumping around" feeling.

Another thing that will become obvious is that much of the search for who I am is spiritual in nature. I've come to see that God is a story, too. Any story about God is bound to have questions, and that's okay—in fact, it's better. All the great answers about God aren't nearly as compelling as the great questions about him.

If you want to go deeper into exploring the spiritual aspect of the stories, I've added references to Bible verses for each point in the disambiguation sections. You don't have to agree with my faith walk to hear my story, and I hope you can read it without feeling forced into a religious box. I'm just convinced that God is an integral part of the search for our identity. It may not be for you, and I respect that. But I also hope you'd at least consider how God can weave his story into yours. It may be life-changing, it certainly was for me.

Before digging into the book, begin with this promise. You are more than you think you are. You're more than the label the world has ascribed to you or is motivating you to adopt. You're unique in all human history, you are the only *you* that will ever exist. Your soul's fingerprint is different from the way everyone describes you—even your fiercest advocates and certainly your harshest critics. You're more than even *you* can imagine. The challenge comes in believing this resolutely enough that you'll let go of the default and begin searching for who you really want to be.

Letting go won't be easy, and it won't just happen. It's a choice you have to make.

The longing to know and live out our identity is evidence that something's off. It's like we misplaced or lost our real identity and have been left with a spare. What if the sense of loss is a sign, a clue intentionally left behind, so we might search for the answer?

My encouragement is to go for the search, give it a chance. What do you have to lose?

These pieces of my story—with their many questions—are an ongoing discovery for me. It's moving and inviting and sometimes provoking and frustrating and scary. I hope you find yourself asking some of the same questions.

Perhaps, as you read, you'll see the pieces of your life differently, you'll see yourself differently. I hope that you'll find you really *do* know who you want to be, you just may not know what to do about it. I hope that knowing *who* you want to be will bring clarity to the roles you play, like a parent, a CEO, a firefighter, a small business owner or a pilot. Or a friend.

I hope.

One thing, though, asking questions will change you, it changes your story. Because once you find out who you want to be, there's no going back.

I wonder what would happen if we all never went back. Maybe there's a way all our stories fit together. Maybe it's not just my story, after all.

Maybe it's our story.

Maybe it's God's story.

Maybe it's history.

A man found an eagle's egg and put it in the nest of a barnyard hen. The eaglet hatched with the brood of chickens and grew up with them.

All his life the eagle did what the barnyard chicks did, thinking he was a barnyard chicken. He scratched the earth for worms and insects. He clucked and cackled. And he would thrash his wings and fly a few feet into the air.

Years passed and the eagle grew very old. One day he saw a magnificent bird above him in the cloudless sky. It glided in graceful majesty among the powerful wind currents, with scarcely a beat of its strong golden wings.

The old eagle looked up in awe. "Who's that?" he asked.

"That's the eagle, the king of the birds," said his neighbor. "He belongs to the sky. We belong to the earth–we're chickens."

So the eagle lived and died a chicken, for that's what he thought he was.

Anthony de Mello, *The Song of the Bird*

PART 1

Beginning the End

To pursue genuine transformation, you must be willing to abandon what has never really worked.

Chapter One

The Identity Strain

If you could see your identity
and hold it in your hand,
what would it look like?

HAVE YOU EVER lost something important?

I lost my bike when I was 12—well, technically, my sister lost it. She borrowed it, and someone stole it when she wasn't looking. I didn't blame her since it wasn't her fault. But man, I really liked that bike. It had a deep golden frame and a white banana seat. It rode smooth and soundless, with no wobbles. I ended up getting another bike, but I don't remember it. I remember the bike I lost more than the bike that replaced it.

Hmm, that's interesting ...

I was 34 when I lost a job for the first time. I was working as an engineer on the B-2 Stealth Bomber, fulfilling my boyhood dream of designing airplanes. The program had come to an end, and everyone was being laid off, well, almost everyone. Since I'd already started shifting toward a ministry career, I wasn't too sad. Still, I loved that job.

I lost my dad to cancer when I was 20. It was the first time someone close to me had died. The finality of it was gut-wrenching. But I was in the thick of engineering classes that didn't allow much bandwidth for grief. I didn't understand the true value of the loss until I was holding Brennan, our firstborn, in my arms. Amid my joy, I imagined how 32 years earlier, Dad had held me in the same way. The weight of the loss rocked me, like when you're standing in the ocean, just offshore in neck-deep water, and a swell hits you unexpectedly. I suddenly had so many questions about how to be a dad—that only a dad can answer.

Recently, I read that Americans lose $56 billion annually to identity fraud. One source really nailed the essence of it: "Identity theft exploits the victim, depriving them of their identity by replacing their reputation with the thief's."

The way the Bible describes it, the same thing happened to us. Humankind, as a species (both male and female), was created in God's image and likeness. We weren't divine, but our nature reflected God in a way that nothing else in the universe did. We were the pinnacle of creation, in perfect relationship with him. Our purpose—to manage creation as God's representatives—flowed out of our identity.

This identity was lost when the first humans believed the Devil's lie that they could be like God. They turned from God and incurred the consequences he'd warned them would come. From this point forward, people were no longer made in *God's* likeness—they were made in *human* likeness. As a result, we now have only hints of what it means to embody the image of our Creator.

Think about it, at a time when creation was young, and humanity had everything to lose, we were robbed. We let our guard down, and the tempter—the thief—slithered in. Our former identity, pristine, uncorrupted by sin and in absolute harmony with God, was craftily and cruelly stolen. And the replacement identity … well, we know what it is, don't we?

Identity theft and losing things like my banana-seat bike, my dream job and my Dad are all good illustrations, but still incomplete. These were familiar and well-known things when they were lost.

But we've never known our lost identity.

Would we even know it if we found it? We might be stepping over it unaware, moving it aside as we reach for something else. It might be hidden in plain sight, right in front of us.

Why are we so compelled to look for something we've never had? And how do we go about finding it?

Who do you want to be?

That question has vexed me, in one way or another, for most of my life. I don't know if this is true for everyone, but for me, this question has a unique spiritual component to it. I remember early in my faith experience reading a verse from the Bible, 2 Corinthians 5:17: "Therefore, if anyone is in Christ, he is a new creation, the old has gone, the new has come!"

Why are we so compelled to look for something we've never had?

This confronted me because I believed myself to be a follower of Christ, and yet I didn't feel new. I was aware of new things, I had made new, genuinely close friends. I had lost the guilt I'd had over not being good enough. I had a new wholesomeness in life and new motivations and goals. But when I looked in the mirror, I still saw the same doubting, skeptical-of-myself self staring back at me.

The weirdest part was that I wasn't fulfilled by being me. Not that I disliked myself, I just was never particularly impressed with myself. I didn't aspire to be me since I didn't really know who "me" was. So, I started trying to be something new by using the most obvious approach, following the rules.

Now I must say, I'm pretty good at the rule thing. If you look at my StrengthsFinder™ profile, I'm even categorized as a "Rule-Follower,"—meaning I value order, process and consistency. As an engineer, I can tell you that everything in the cosmos usually fits into a pattern, follows a law, is determined by a formula or can be generalized by a rule. Not to be overly rigid, that's simply the order of things (just ask any engineer, they'll tell you so!).

I went from following my own rules to following a new set of reformed, Christian rules—most of which, coincidentally, start with "don't." The Christian paradigm tips quickly toward reacting to sin. So, Christians seem to have a really good idea about what they're *not* supposed to be—correction, what they're not supposed to *do*.

I went along in this mode for a while and was pretty content. I was learning many new things and having some wonderful experiences. But after a while, I discovered the same old weirdness was still there. I still wasn't overly impressed with my new self.

All of my shortcomings, foibles and unsatisfied longings were evidence that something was missing, and I couldn't put my finger on it. It had nothing to do with activity, relationships, status, education, or any other external stuff in my life—all the stuff I always thought counted for something.

Change is more a matter of who we are than what we do, it's more about identity than activity.

It had everything to do with identity. I could mimic the behavior of other people I knew and respected, but there's no way to mimic an identity. I didn't know how to be me because I didn't know who "me" should be.

It became clear that genuine transformation—change—is more a matter of who we are than what we do, it's more about identity than activity.

I can identify with Flick in *A Bug's Life,* and his pity party after his spectacularly public failure gets him banished from the ant colony: "Let's face it the colony's right: I just make things worse. That bird is a guaranteed failure—just like me."

You may wrestle with other things, but the self-talk "voice" I've heard loudest and most often in my life is the one who accuses me of being a failure. It's an ever-present companion that wonders aloud about my potential to succeed. It predicts ominous, crash-and-burn outcomes, then faithfully confirms with *I told you so* judgments when I don't accomplish the goal. Every success brings the reminder that even a broken watch is right twice a day.

"Can you measure up?"

"Will you make others proud or be a disappointment?"

"Don't screw this up!"

"Are you sure you want to do that?"

"You're being lazy."

"People will laugh at you if you get it wrong."

"See, you missed the mark—yet again!"

Interacting with the voice actually feels normal, almost comforting, in a sick way. It's *so* easy to believe. It feels almost authoritative like it *really* knows what it's talking about. It's easy to develop a kind of codependency on it. I know it's unhealthy, but I don't know what life would be like without it. It's *always* been there for me, giving me attention and input when I needed it.

My inner voice mixes with the inputs of the world around me, uncertainty, greed, fear, jealousy, discrimination, judgment, exploitation, materialism, and productivity ... It masterfully confuses and clouds my search for who I want to be. It presses and pulls me to leverage and protect my self-interests. It's like gravity, the bigger the issue, the stronger the pull.

At this point in my life, the voice is mostly an annoyance I've learned to tune out. Wisdom, experience and truth disarm the sting of its accusations. But it takes effort to resist, and sometimes I don't. And when I don't, of course, it *always* reminds me.

My friend Lee's earliest childhood memory was being left at the orphanage at five years old and watching his dad drive away. His mom had died, and his dad couldn't take care of him. Lee was put into foster care, where he was emotionally and physically abused, which led to alcohol and drugs and breaking all the rules. He left "home" at 16 as an alcoholic and was homeless until he joined the Army, where things got really interesting. Because, as we all know, there are hardly any rules in the Army.

Lee has a redemption side to his story that's as beautiful as the broken side is horrific. But it's still hard for him to shake the feeling of being abandoned. Loss of relationships and community is tougher for him than for most people. Anytime it happens, he fights against feelings of being devalued and unlovable.

There are so many other stories. The girl whose mother was always critical of every move she made. In her teens she turned to guys for affection and acceptance, but the only thing she got from them was pregnant. Or the guy with the perfectionistic father who pushed him so hard to excel that even success wasn't good enough. He grew up without the belief that it was even possible to accept yourself as you are. So many stories.

We trust imperfect and limited people to define a sacred, holy and invisible quality.

We've all been shaped by family, friends and peers who've influenced us—especially in our formative years. Maybe they aren't as extreme as Lee's, or maybe they were positive influences instead of destructive ones. Many of us have a version of statements like "You always … " or "You'll never … " that we've held onto for years. They're the ones we heard repeatedly and now often repeat to ourselves. These words shape our self-perception like a chisel carves an image out of stone, creating an identity that now drives our behavior.

But what if we're more than that self-perception? More than what other people think about us?

It's telling that we rely so heavily on others for feedback on who we are. We use relationships like mirrors. Our parents, siblings, friends, teachers, coaches—even our heroes and antagonists—all reflect an image of our identity back to us. The quality of the image varies based on the people reflecting it. Some are good mirrors. Others are cracked and broken and reflect a skewed and fragmented image.

It comes down to this. We trust imperfect and limited people to define a sacred, holy and invisible quality. That other people's words are powerful is obvious. The bigger, deeper question is: Why? Why is *their* perception *of* us so important *to us*?

So here we are, straining to find a formless identity. Fumbling and bumbling through expectations, relationships, career aspirations and life goals. We step on each other's toes and trip over our own feet as we offend and misunderstand and disappoint and take advantage of one another. All in a world that distracts and pulls us toward evil.

Straining.

We're driven to disprove the unspoken lie that we are the events of our past, or—even worse—we believe it and act out accordingly.

We strive for achievement to compensate or distract us from the terrifying prospect that we might actually be who we think we are.

We spend energy trying to be the fantasy person we think we should be—or *someone else* thinks we should be. We succumb to what Felicia Wu Song calls "the industrialization of you and me," our assimilation in the collective of the digital world. This process is like the Borg in Star Trek, the Next Generation. The Borg are alien cyborgs who achieve victory and domination by assimilating people into "the Collective," the combined intelligence of all its subjects who were linked together into a hive mind. But in the assimilation, the subjects lose their individual identity and become drones of the Collective. Contemporary digital identity has a similar assimilation process in play, where we lose our sense of self and self-worth as the Collective tells us who we are and who we should be—whether we know it or not, whether we like it or not.[1]

We experiment with being different people in the hopes that one of them might fit.

We're either straining to be someone we're not or straining to *not* be someone we think we *are*.

Or we're so afraid or intimidated by the question that we bury it in the back of the junk drawer of our life and try not to think about it.

So we work hard to cope and compensate. We try to be kind and live by the Golden Rule. We consume books and videos and self-help and religious activities and community programs—that all leave us unfulfilled. And we know all this is not as it should be.

We work to reclaim a long-lost, true identity that we know only by the shape of the hole it left in our souls. The 17th-century French mathematician, Blaise Pascal, captured the essence of the loss when he said, "There is a God-shaped vacuum in the heart of each [person] which cannot be satisfied by any created thing but only by God the Creator." There's an itch in our soul just beyond our reach to scratch, a splinter in our mind we can't quite locate. All this in a world promising status and technology and information and science and wealth can remove all the mystery and numb the longing we have to fill our void.

As I consider it all, a conviction settles over me. It's a quest—I want to experience the promise in that verse that confronted me so long ago to be "a new creation," where "the old has gone, the new has come." If, as promised, I am a new creation—one the world has never seen—I want to discover what it means to *be* that creation in my space and time. I want to embody this unique piece of God's story that he's writing *through me*. I believe it can be found, that it's meant to be found. I want to find it.

Are you who you want to be?

It's a big question, isn't it?

In my experience, most people don't think about it, at least not out loud, which makes sense because it's challenging to answer, not so much because it's hard or complicated but because it's so … final.

What if our answer is "no"? What if our answer is "yes," and we don't like who that person is? And, for that matter, why does it seem like a question that has a right and a wrong answer? Why does dismissing the question as irrelevant feel so dissatisfying?

If you can't answer the question right away, I get it. It's not exactly a conversation starter. It's a philosophical, introspective and deeply personal question. To many people, it's an impractical one, it doesn't help pay the bills or get that project done or figure out what to eat today.

My guess is you've thought about identity, at least a little bit, without realizing it. You just called it other things, like choosing a new hobby or career path or a marriage partner or sexual preference. These are more tangible, present and practical. But those topics are ultimately driven by the question of identity, along with its companion question of identifying our life's purpose.

Identity is our sense of self. It's the compass heading that life aligns with–or doesn't align with.

Identity is our sense of self. It's the compass heading that life aligns with—or doesn't align with. When there's alignment, we feel fulfilled, directed and on point. When there isn't, we feel disoriented and frustrated, like all of life's efforts are taking us down some rabbit trail.

And how can you really know?

"Are you who you want to be" is an orientation question, or rather, a *re*-orientation question. Answering it could change the trajectory of your life.

Heck, for that matter, just *asking* it could.

DISAMBIGUATION
CHAPTER 1

THE BIG IDEA:

We've lost our created identity and don't know how to find it. And to make matters worse, we don't even know what it looks like.

IDENTITY IS OUR SENSE OF SELF.

It's who we perceive ourselves to be (or think we should be). It's closely tied to purpose. Identity (who we are) informs purpose (why we exist). Knowing our identity brings clarity and simplicity to life. Not knowing it makes life chaotic and rudderless, with no point of reference to navigate by.[2]

OUR ORIGINAL IDENTITY WAS LOST.

We were the Creator's sons and daughters, having many of his qualities (except for his divinity). But mankind's spiritual enemy (Satan) convinced us we could be more, and we fell for it. This "Fall" corrupted mankind and all of creation. We've never known our original identity–though we're keenly aware of its loss. We sense that a connection with God is possible. We just don't know who he is and where to find him. [3]

IT'S HARD TO SEARCH FOR OUR TRUE IDENTITY IN A BROKEN WORLD.

The social world we live in–its values, principles, ways, priorities, etc.–is under Satan's influence. He actively disrupts, deceives and interferes with our attempts to find our lost identity. We've also inherited a sinful nature called "The flesh" that entices us toward evil and will not sponsor or help us discover our original identity.[4]

WE SEEK CONFIRMATION OF OUR LOST IDENTITY THROUGH RELATIONSHIPS.

Since we're communal beings, this is a good principle. But this, too, was corrupted in the Fall. Now we depend upon imperfect people to define what can only be accurately and completely defined by a loving, divine Father-Creator.[5]

LIFE ITSELF IS THE SEARCH FOR OUR LOST IDENTITY.

Without it, we'll never be satisfied or rightly oriented. Our values will be incomplete, our character will be malleable and uneven. We'll have an elusive sense of purpose, and so we'll live in a state of unfulfilled longings and not know why.[6]

Chapter Two

The Caramel Apple

How do you become … *you*?

ONE FALL, WHEN our kids were young, we got some caramel apples at a school fundraiser. Sometime later, Brennan (who was about eight at the time) was foraging for snacks and found the last one in a kitchen cabinet. Of course, when you're a kid, and you find a caramel apple, you're not concerned that it was in a cabinet instead of the refrigerator. You also don't bring up the good news with Mom, otherwise, you'd have to share it with your siblings.

The caramel coating was in fine condition. Sadly, the apple was not, and it actually fell off the stick when he picked it up—a warning sign that somehow escaped his attention. Undeterred, he chomped into it and immediately realized his treat had turned into a trick.

Hmm … come to think of it, I've never seen Brennan eat another caramel apple.

Do you know how some experiences in life stand out more than others? How some events can be portals to a deeper level of truth or reality? This one stood out to me. The more I thought about Brennan's caramel apple, the more I began to see life—and myself—in a new way.

It's easy to pay attention to the externals in life, like our appearance, our weight, our clothes, cars, houses and life's accessories, so to speak. We tend to give energy toward things others see. Not that this is wrong, but it's out of proportion—or rather, out of order. Because if the apple is good, the caramel elevates the goodness. But the best caramel in the world can't improve an apple that's in bad shape.

The best caramel in the world can't improve an apple that's in bad shape.

What's inside matters most.

How do you describe yourself to other people? I'd never really thought about this question until the caramel apple, then I couldn't stop thinking about it. I started listening to how other people describe themselves in the so-tell-me-about-yourself conversations.

"I'm a homemaker."

"I'm in sales."

"I'm a sports fan."

"I'm Italian."

"I'm a Republican/Democrat/Independent."

"I'm a golfer."

"I'm a [INSERT COLLEGE MASCOT HERE]."

"I'm an artist."

"I'm a husband and father of three."

I suspect that most of us realize these things aren't who we are. They're what we do, what we associate or identify with. It can be frustrating to think about it. Saying "I'm in sales" is, at best, just a slice of who we are. But we say it anyway because that's what's expected. Going further would be weird.

The *so-tell-me-about-yourself* conversation feels like dancing. If you can dance and you enjoy it, this may not be a great analogy for you. But for me, dancing is an awkward experience.

I think it's because my old girlfriend was a terrific dancer. She moved and flowed like a mountain stream in the spring thaw. Effortless. Powerful and purposeful. Every time I tried to dance, I thought it looked more like a seizure, sort of herky-jerky.

She always looked for opportunities to dance. I always avoided them. But when you're dating, you sometimes have to get out on the floor together. Out I'd lurch, feeling fortunate I didn't have to dance alone, watching her and marveling at how a human body could move like that.

Years after that relationship ended, my buddy David set me up on a blind date with a friend from college named Cheryl. "She's a neat gal," he promised. "You'll really like her." Do you know what we did on that blind date? We went country dancing with a group from church.

Great, what a way to meet a neat gal.

David and Cheryl both went to Texas A&M, where people identify themselves as Aggies. The campus is in College Station, a small town in southeast Texas where country dancing is nearly a way of life. Cheryl loves to dance and went dancing frequently while she was there.

She came prepared for our blind date, dressed up in her frilly shirt and lizard-skin boots. On the other hand, I had no Western clothes or boots, so I wore my Topsiders. Barefoot, we were the same height, but not that night. I felt six inches shorter than her. Not very confidence-inspiring.

We stepped out onto the dance floor, and I was instantly, brutally uncomfortable. I tried to lead because that's what guys do in dancing. But I had no idea what I was doing. At least the height issue went away quickly because I spent most of my time looking at my feet, willing them to move in sync with hers. It didn't work too well.

Well, okay … it didn't work at all.

Finally, we decided it'd be best if she led around the floor—talk about humiliating. She could have made it embarrassing for me, but she didn't. Besides, she was happy just to be dancing.

As it turns out, the whole dance thing actually broke a whole lot of ice. After all, blind dates can be awkward. And my first impression of her wasn't very good—she was too tall, and I wasn't into country music or dancing. She wasn't too impressed with me either. But I think it set us up for truly, genuinely, desperately falling in love.

But that's a story for another time.

Meeting people is a lot like me trying to dance. There's an awkward herky-jerkiness that often gets in the way. We're not really sure who the other person is, and we're even less sure about being vulnerable enough to talk about who we are—If we even know *how* to talk about who we are.

So, to avoid the awkwardness, we talk about what we do, like jobs, hobbies, interests … the externals, the accessories. This isn't necessarily bad. I think what we do is important. But there's more to us than what we do, right?

It's a shame that getting past the surface of our activity is so unwieldy. It's like we're stepping on each other's toes when we know we could be more in sync. When it comes to knowing who we are and knowing each other, we don't dance well.

If we even know *how* to talk about who we are.

If we knew how to dance, dancing wouldn't be as much work. There'd be an ease to it, a natural flow. We'd know how to talk about ourselves. We'd know how to listen to others, how to ask them about who they really are as people. We wouldn't step on each other's stories. And if we weren't so worried about what other people think of our dancing, we wouldn't be so self-conscious.

There's a difference between dancing and being a dancer. Dancers know how to dance. It's not so much about doing it. It's a natural outflow of who they are. Dancers dance because they're dancers. Dancing fits them like their smile or their laugh.

That's the way I imagine dancing could be … when I imagine being a dancer.

If you're an American, what do you *do* to *be* an American?

I fly the Stars and Stripes in front of my house. I put it out every day … well, almost every day. I don't put it out when it rains because a wet flag in our living room is quite a mess. And sometimes, I forget when things get busy. So in truth, I don't put it out *every* day. But I intend to.

I like apple pie, quite a lot, in fact. But I've reached the age where apple pie tends to tarry longer on the waist. So I don't eat it much anymore. And I really love a good hot dog, although it's hard to stop at just one—eating one quickly turns into eating three.

Then there's baseball, the great American pastime. Though I never had the hand-eye coordination for it, I appreciate watching a great hitter work the count or a great pitcher work the strike zone. Though I think the games are too long and often boring, there's something very American about players chewing bubble gum and eating sunflower seeds in a major sport.

I practice or identify with these very American things. But they aren't what makes me an American. I know other countries have baseball, apple pie and even hot dogs, but somehow, I doubt these make their citizens feel American.

When we lived in Canada, I asked my Canadian friends what it meant to be a Canadian. They didn't quite know how to answer (a clue that it's a very American question). They finally boiled it down to two things. One was hockey, the great Canadian game. I can't say that every Canadian loves hockey because I haven't met every Canadian. But I can say that every Canadian I've met loves hockey—passionately.

The second thing my friends said was that being Canadian means that you're not American. I, uh, … wasn't quite sure how to take that.

What do you *do* to *be* spiritual?

It seems that there are lots of options on the table. At a local conference a while back, a fellow St. Petersburg resident told me about her experience with dolphins swimming near her dock. She said putting a megaphone into the water and making low-frequency "oohing" sounds gave her a special connection with them, it made her feel very spiritual.

"Wow, " I said. "That's interesting. Do they ever talk back?"

"Well, I don't know, because I don't speak dolphin," she said a little reprovingly, as if I should have realized she couldn't speak dolphin. "But they do seem really curious about what I'm doing."

"I can imagine … ," I added.

She then went into a long discussion about how she serves others.

"I make people laugh."

"No kidding!" I said too quickly to block an unintended tone of sarcasm. "Tell me more about it."

She then pulled a red clown nose out of her purse and put it on. I found this really distracting and started wondering where this conversation was going.

"I go to nursing homes," she continued, "or birthday parties, anywhere I can spread a little joy."

To my relief, she soon took off the nose. But as she continued to talk, she started moving closer and getting more animated, bobbing her head and waving her arms. She even put a hand on my shoulder at one point. I quickly went from being distracted to uncomfortable.

For a moment, I thought she was going to ask me to dance.

I leaned backward, which she apparently interpreted as an invitation to move closer. Then I began stepping backward.

She continued, unfazed by my retreat, "There's something very freeing and uplifting when you practice laughter … "

By now, she was so close her facial features were blurry—way too close for comfort. I had some papers in my hand, which I tried to use as a barrier by also crossing my arms. It didn't work.

" … I think it makes us one when we laugh together."

I can't remember what I said, but I brought the conversation to a close and began looking for the quickest way out of the room. As I said goodbye, she gave me a hug and a big smile, which I returned with as much authenticity as I could muster.

I felt genuinely torn. I appreciated her intention, her innocent passion for what she believed to be spiritual and her commitment to helping people. On the other hand, I couldn't help but find her approach intrusive. And her view of spirituality was … well, different from mine.

I didn't want to judge her because I do think it's good to laugh together and connect with nature. And I think dolphins are really cool, though I feel no engagement with them at a spiritual level.

The experience made me wonder how I appear when I start talking about how I practice *my* faith. Do I seem off the edge of the map? Do I distract them from seeing God as I understand him? I wonder if they feel like my Canadian friends who don't want to be American because of the way Americans act.

I hope not.

It's easy to think of spirituality in terms of activity. Whether it's *oohing* to dolphins or attending church, deeper spirituality often looks like something we do.

Christians have their own unique flavor of "doing"—which is curious since it's a faith system based on trust and relationship. I regularly encountered this during the 15 years I served as a vocational pastor. People searching for a deeper faith experience would inevitably say, "I just want to know what God wants me to do." It was as if God had some kind of top-secret assignment, and it was their job to discover it.

God had some kind of top-secret assignment, and it was their job to discover it.

I wonder if doing things is what God desires most. Not that doing things is unimportant. But if doing things is the answer, why are we still asking the question, "what does God want me to do?"

It's like my life with Cheryl. I could take a checklist approach to relate with her. At the top of the list might be telling her daily that I love her. Next could be taking 15 minutes a day to listen to whatever she has to say without offering an opinion or solution. Date nights would also make the list, but they can't include watching a movie with stuff blowing up and selling her on the idea that it's a love story. Long walks on the beach are more in order.

Dancing is an option, but only if I'm really desperate.

The checklist approach might work fine for a while. But eventually, she'd realize my affection is dutiful, my intimacy regimented. Love isn't based on productivity metrics. Doing stuff with her works when it's the fruit of the relationship, not the means to it. I don't get to love by doing the stuff on the list. I do the stuff on the list because I'm in love.

When you think about it, trying to be spiritual by doing stuff is like trying to be an American by eating hot dogs and singing the national anthem. What makes us think that our performance in all the spiritual activities will make us spiritual?

I think productivity is fine and even necessary in many cases. It's good to incentivize, reward and celebrate production and accomplishment. But in a world that worships at the altar of productivity, we can artificially inflate the value of what we do and what we produce.

In focusing solely on what we do externally, we neglect who we are internally. Ultimately, we end up with two versions of ourselves—one inside and another outside. Living one life is challenging enough, why try to live two? How can an approach that promises double-mindedness and hypocrisy be fruitful? How does this help us be more effective in the roles we play? How can we influence others for good if we're misaligned?

In my opinion, spirituality should make a person whole and complete. If that could come through doing things on a list, we'd have figured it out by now. We'd have come up with a list that everyone would agree on, a universal recipe to follow.

Living one life is challenging enough, why try to live two?

But we haven't.

Even within Christianity—a faith system with a clear and widely agreed perspective of God and humanity—we can't agree on a list. We've created different lists and then judged each other's lists. We have list-pride and list-hate. Even when we're nice about it, our lists have divided us, whether or not we're willing to admit it.

What if the things we do or don't do, while relevant, are just the caramel coating of our identity? What if there's something going on (or not going on) in our core, would we know it? How would we know it? And would we be willing to change to be able to know it?

The question "What does God want me to do" is relevant. But what if there's a different question we should ask—one that we should ask *first*?

"Who does God want me to *be*?"

This question began to reveal itself when I was pretty far into my identity strain. The more I asked the question above, the more I realized that what I was doing to be spiritual wasn't working. I began to see that my practices and activity—my spiritual work ethic, if you will—was an Outside-In approach. Do, in order to be.

This Outside-In approach is based on the "we become what we do" mantra. It's an empowering idea and sells well in productivity-oriented cultures. Like a New Year's resolution, it actually worked for a season of life.

But then March came, and it wasn't producing the difference I'd anticipated. There were qualities of life I longed for that my Outside-In approach couldn't deliver. Peace, for example. "Peace be with you," Jesus said. " … my peace I give to you. I do not give to you as the world gives. Do not let your hearts be troubled and do not be afraid."[7]

Jesus talked of peace as if it should be alive, beating like my heart and flowing through me like the blood in my veins. That simply wasn't my experience. Whatever "peace" I had seemed … manufactured.

Talking about peace was like talking about Venice or Istanbul, or some other interesting place I knew existed but never actually visited. It was as if I was vicariously trying to relive someone else's vacation and call it my own. The more I talked about peace, the more I became aware of a profound lack of it. My identity was not peaceful.

Love is another example. Could I identify so completely with Jesus' unconditional love for me that I surrendered the need for collateral, quid-pro-quo love from others? Could I live so intimately, presently and trustingly in *his* love that I expected and required nothing in return for *mine*? Was I able to love someone who *couldn't* love me back? Or who *wouldn't* love me back? And to love not just because it's a task to accomplish but simply because it's right?

Loving others unconditionally is the most difficult thing I've ever tried to do. Frankly, I'm not sure I've ever done it in my life.

Not even once.

While this may sound depressing, finally realizing I was on a dead-end street was actually quite liberating. I came to see that the problem wasn't my *performance*, like I didn't try hard enough to love others or to be at peace.

Instead of an ethic, I needed an ethos.

The real problem was my *orientation*. If I don't change who I am at my core, any Outside-In change in my work ethic is only a new layer of caramel coating. To see the evidence of genuine peace and love in my life, I had to become a loving and peaceful person. Instead of an ethic, I needed an ethos.

This required a completely different approach, Inside-out. Be, in order to do.

I can't tell you how it happened. Maybe it was a night I couldn't go to sleep. Maybe it was on a beach walk with Cheryl, watching the horizon devour an ever-ambering sun. Maybe it wasn't a singular, ah-ha moment at all, but a series of moments that came together like pearls on a string. I don't know how or when it happened.

But it happened.

I became aware of a question rolling around in the corners of my mind.

What if God doesn't want me to "do" *anything?*

"That's loony," I responded to myself. "What do you mean, 'not do anything?'"

"Well, what if who you are *is God's top priority? How would your life change if you focused all your attention on that?"*

"Well, of course … it's important to know who I am."

"C'mon, you don't even know what you're saying! If knowing who you are is so important, what difference has it made in your life?

"Well, uh, ... "

"Exactly! You only focus on what you do. What if you focus instead on who you are—identity first, not activity?

"Are you nutsoid? 'Identity first' ... that sounds like psychobabble. Knowing what to do—having a plan of action—has always worked. Look at how far it's taken me!"

"Yeah, frustrating, isn't it? C'mon, I know the 'do' thing is how the world works. I know it's how you've always done everything you've ever done. But what if there's a better way?

"Get over it, Don Quixote. I'm not abandoning my whole approach to life. That's crazy talk, too many unknowns."

But then, a pause, a doubt. *What if he's right?*

"Okay, I think I get what you're saying. But maybe we should work on doing *and* being at the same time, just to be safe."

"That's a compromise. If we don't make identity a priority, we'll keep it on the back burner—and you know it. C'mon, man, it's an all-in thing. Get in or get out. Go big or go home."

There was more reflection as I thought about how to answer myself. But it didn't help. I had no reply that made any sense. My interlocutor sensed my hesitation and jumped on it.

"What if? What if God knows something we don't? What if he knows that through discovering who we should be, *we'll know what we should* do? *And what if he knows that if we focus too much on what we should* do, *we'll never discover who we should* be?"

"You need to let me think on this one. You know once we go this way, we can't go back, right?"

"Yeah, I know. But there's gotta be a way to think about identity that is genuinely Inside-Out. God-centered, without it defaulting to an Outside-In approach. I can't help but think that if we live Inside-Out, we'd save so many people from frustration and guilt and loneliness and mediocrity."

Another pause and a faraway look.

"I think we'd save so many more people."

"I said you need to let me think!"

"Well, the way I see it we can't wait until we get comfortable with the idea, 'cause we never will. We just have to go for it."

Weirdly, this was all starting to make sense. But it was still too far out to get my mind around, much less my heart. It's asking a lot to focus on identity over activity. And I wasn't sure where to begin.

"So what would it take to convince you that God really is more concerned about our identity? What do we have to lose?"

"Oh, I don't know. Maybe everything I've ever known about myself and about life!"

"Well ... couldn't that be a good thing?"

DISAMBIGUATION
CHAPTER 2

THE BIG IDEA:

We usually rely on our external environment to define our internal identity. This approach is ultimately doomed to fail, and the results are short-lived at best.

WHAT'S ON THE INSIDE MATTERS MOST.

When our internal self is centered, stable and peaceful, we can be healthy–even if our external environment is not. But the opposite is simply not true. If our internal life is in turmoil, we will never be healthy, even with an ideal external life. [8]

WE ARE NOT WHAT WE DO.

The things that identify us externally (roles, causes, hobbies, achievements, acts of kindness, etc.) are *what we do*, not *who we are*. They don't identify who we are on the inside.[9]

IT'S POSSIBLE TO BE ONE PERSON ON THE OUTSIDE AND A DIFFERENT PERSON ON THE INSIDE.

When our internal and external lives are misaligned, we become double-minded, inconsistent and hypocritical. We can't live in this condition for very long before it becomes unfruitful and potentially destructive to us and those around us–especially if we're in a position of influence, like a parent, friend, teacher or leader.[10]

OUR DEFAULT, OUTSIDE-IN APPROACH MUST BE ABANDONED IN FAVOR OF AN INSIDE-OUT APPROACH.

External actions and how we engage with the world around us are like caramel coating. Our identity is like the apple. An Outside-In approach focuses on the coating and can't really change what's at the core. The Inside-Out approach focuses on internal transformation, which then drives what we do. Our behavior becomes the product of our identity.[11]

LIVING INSIDE-OUT CAN BE DISORIENTING IN THE BEGINNING.

Action-oriented people may find it an unproductive waste of time. Introspective people may get overanalytical and stuck. But continue to embrace the dissatisfaction from knowing your Outside-In approach hasn't worked. The knowledge of a better way and the steps to take will reveal themselves soon enough.[12]

Chapter Three

The Fishbowl

What's keeping you from
being who you really want to be?

How do you *become* who you want to be? How do you actually *get* there?

Knowing how to *get* to the destination is almost as important as knowing the destination. On the one hand, not knowing your destination makes you a random sightseer—could be fun, but in the end, you're still lost. On the other hand, not knowing how to get to your destination can leave you frustrated, fatigued and wondering if getting there is really worth it.

The first time I ever drove in Boston was back in the day, before Google Maps and turn-by-turn navigation on my phone. I was rudely awakened to the aggressiveness of drivers in Boston when I left Logan International. Seven lanes of traffic narrowed quickly down to two going into the Ted Williams Tunnel. I didn't know that the Boston driving mantra was, "I was here first, pal," and that a turn signal meant, "Please cut me off."

Once through the tunnel, I was on to my goal of seeing the historic sites. But I hadn't counted on the fact that the streets were laid out 100 years *before* the American Revolution. I had a map (remember those?) for all the good it did me. Nothing was parallel to anything else. Even the city blocks were curved. I wanted to see the location of the Boston Tea Party but drove past it multiple times. Every time I thought I was there, I couldn't actually get there. Then I'd come to a traffic circle. The confluence of cars from six directions felt more like a NASCAR qualifier than organized traffic.

I knew where I wanted to go in Boston but didn't know how to get there. I told my friend Rick about my experience. He's a fellow resident of St. Petersburg and a native Bostonian who still pronounces "harbor" as "hahbah." He just smiled at me. *Toughen up, bucko.*

Admittedly, I felt like a wimp for bringing it up. But it really frustrated me to see Boston yet not really see it. It was so close and yet so far away. And to this day, I'd be no help to anyone trying to find their way around Boston, which is a shame because it's important to help someone else on their journey.

When I think about the question, "Are you who you want to be?" the first thing that sticks to the wall of my mind is the word "want." It's alarmingly easy to want things, isn't it?

There's a difference between wanting and *really wanting*. The first is a craving, like wanting a cheeseburger (though my vegan friends may need a different analogy). There are a number of really good local hamburger restaurants in St. Pete, like Engine No. 9, The Job Site and The Bier Boutique. Our current go-to is The Burg, a hole-in-the-wall joint on Central Avenue just outside of downtown. I usually go for the Build Your Own, the eight-ounce patty with blue cheese, grilled onions and bacon on a brioche bun. It's big and juicy, and they provide lots of napkins.

The second, *really wanting*, is more of a yearning. It's marrow-deep, profound, right and good, a holy desire. It's like the longing to be loved or to be free or to belong. It's so strong that sometimes it aches.

I'm not sure what to call this *want*. I'm not even sure it should be named. Giving it a name might cheapen it. Some of life's experiences assure me that this *want* exists, but only in glimpses and flashes. I sense it in experiences like my daughter's smile or a big, hearty laugh shared with friends, or a long, wet kiss. Or maybe a perfectly timed afternoon nap. In a hammock. In a cool breeze. After a big lunch. Or the view from the top of a mountain where the air is virgin, and the sky has no end.

This *want* is so deep that I sense it in my conscience when I slow down enough to listen. The conscience is like a Wayfinder, and it doesn't drive, it only points. In this case, my conscience points to a Great Satisfaction that I sense is coming. Though I don't know when, I know something *is* coming, something as deep and profound and timeless as this *want* that resists being named.

Sometimes, when I'm yearning for this unnamed *want*, I turn to the simpler, cheeseburger want to fulfill it. I can see this cheap substitution coming, as predictable as the plot in a Hallmark movie. I keep telling myself that this is a classic quick fix. I know it'll only distract me for the briefest of moments, which only heightens the depth of the *want* that can't be named.

We long for the profound and eternal, but we settle for the cheap and temporary.

But I do it anyway. I eat cheeseburgers to get to paradise.

I marvel at the simplicity of the cheeseburger want, and the power it has over us. What is it about this want that makes people of all walks and intelligence levels exchange their reputations, careers and families for a moment of cheeseburger heaven? How can the United States be one of the most affluent countries on the planet with more access to consumable happiness than anyone in the history of mankind, and also have one of the highest rates of clinical depression in the world?

We long for the profound and eternal, but we settle for the cheap and temporary. It's as if we can see where we want to go, but there's something we can't see that's preventing us from getting there.

My friends Kerri and Coco once told me about an experience with their mobile service provider.

"We *hate* them!"

"Really?" I asked, surprised by her reaction. "How come?"

"It's so frustrating! You wouldn't believe it … " She continued to explain how she'd ordered two new phones, but the company actually set up two additional phone *numbers*. When she called to correct it, she got a man in a call center somewhere in India who was more than happy to fix her problem.

"Yes ma'am, we can cancel the phone numbers. All you need to do is sign up for an extended contract."

"Uh, excuse me?"

"Yes ma'am, we will not charge the penalty if you extend your contract for another two years. That way, you won't have to pay for canceling your service with us."

"But I'm not canceling service. I already have two numbers, I don't need two more. I'm asking you to fix a mistake *you* made."

"Yes ma'am, I understand. But if you'll just agree to extend the contract, there won't be any additional charges."

Round and around, they went. No matter what she said, she couldn't make the logic stick in his head.

"He wasn't talking to me," Kerri realized. "His answers didn't match my questions. He was reading from a script, and my questions weren't in his script."

Coco was equally livid about another issue. "All I wanted was to activate the new phone *they sent me*!

"No problem, sir." He recounted his conversation with another agent. "We'll just need to ask you a security question to verify your identity. Can you tell us your favorite sport?"

Coco is from Peru, where there's one universal favorite sport.

"Soccer," he confidently proclaimed.

"I'm sorry sir, that doesn't match the answer we have on our records."

"Well, there's no other sport I even know how to play."

"I'm sorry sir, that doesn't match our records."

"Okay, is there some other way to verify I am the owner? I've had my service with you for years, and this is the same number I've always had. I don't ever remember answering any 'favorite sport' question, and if I did, I would have said 'soccer.'"

"I'm sorry sir, that doesn't match our records. So, there's nothing we can do. But I hope you have a nice day, okay?"

There have been seasons where I was convinced God clearly didn't get the big idea behind customer service. I called him, expecting a level of service, then felt like my questions didn't match the answers on his script.

I ended up with a grudge against God for not serving me. I felt stuck in a contract with the only service provider around. I was tempted to think he wasn't really the God I thought he was, or maybe he was finicky or too busy. Then came the thought that he was punishing me for something I'd done wrong, which made me feel guilty for even asking him for help.

Sometimes I had both the grudge and the guilt at the same time—which doesn't make any sense because those two positions don't reconcile. One has to be true, and the other has to be false.

Or what if they're both false?

It's all so confusing. As a faithful customer, I expected a base level of value-added service in the relationship. If I had given less to God, I wouldn't have expected so much. *What the heck is God doing? Doesn't he know the power of a good referral? Doesn't he want to strengthen his customer base? Increase his market share?*

There have been seasons where I was convinced God clearly didn't get the big idea behind customer service.

My mom died a little over 10 years ago. She was a wonderful mom. Not perfect by any stretch, but wonderful just the same. She developed throat cancer, and for the last 10 months of her life, she couldn't speak because of the tracheostomy tube. Normal life for her meant breathing through a small tube that stuck out below her larynx. It required frequent suctioning to clear the congestion. Most of that time, she was unable to swallow or blow her nose. She had to constantly swab the saliva that dripped out the corners of her mouth. She couldn't taste food or her beloved coffee as she fed herself through another tube connected to her stomach.

Through it all, she remained beautiful and gracious. Although she never complained or asked for pity, and although she never once hinted at feeling sorry for herself, it must have been a miserable experience. "Normal" for her had become endless hours of bodily maintenance. Even when we were with her, there was little conversation. She was profoundly alone, a castaway on the island of her thoughts.

I wonder if she had forgotten what it was like to be satisfied with a meal or to engage in conversation with friends. For her, cloistered in an existence that was not what it should have been, the abnormal had become normal.

I'm convinced there's a similar process in play with the spiritual aspect of our identity search. I wonder if we've forgotten how to breathe deep, to taste and smell God. Being trapped in a consumerist existence, what shouldn't be normal, has become normal. As good and faithful customers, we carry the ego and expectation that God should reward our religious duty to him with exceptional customer service and deliver on our deepest wants. Sensing he hasn't, we turn to cheeseburger wants.

I'm amazed at how deep this consumer mindset goes in my own life. It's a despicable foe, going underground and using guerilla warfare tactics. It's increasingly subversive and relentless. It lives in the not-yet-sanctified shadows of my soul, strengthening itself in the moonless nights of my fatigue or failure. It's emboldened by self-pity and it's opportunistic in seasons of challenge or uncertainty. I've tried hard to steel myself against it, to act and talk differently, but it is still there in my heart.

What shouldn't be normal, has become normal.

And it keeps me from where I long to go.

I have to ask myself: Am I—my consumerist, have-it-my-way self—my own invisible barrier to the life I can't get to? Am I willing to admit I'm so caught up in a life I lust for that I drive right by the life I truly, desperately *want?* Can I stop falling for the trick of believing life's fancy widgets and titles and opportunities and happiness will provide what I need most?

If God were offering genuine transformation, would I see it for what it was? How would I distinguish it from the frustrations and disappointments of life not going the way I expected? Am I so myopically focused on what God can do *for* me that I'm blind to what he wants to do *in* me? Or *through* me? Am I willing to accept that God may want to partner with me in discovering an identity he's designed, one that my self-determination can't see—much less produce?

My conscience convinces me there's a paradise in this life, a place of fulfillment and peace that has nothing to do with cheeseburgers. I've also come to see that, in so many ways, I am my own barrier to experiencing it. I think this paradise is a foretaste, an appetizer to an eventual main entrée.

That paradise, by the way, is where I believe Mom is now, based on what she said when she could still speak. I believe she's gone past the barrier to life beyond the life she lived when she was with us. She's in a new normal now.

I wonder what *that* paradise is like?

Have you ever looked at fish in a bowl? I wonder how it must feel to see a life you can't get to, no matter how hard you swim toward it. The other life is clear to see. The barrier is not.

I had lived a life trapped in a prison of doing and quick-fix wants. My own Outside-In approach was the barrier keeping me from going where I wanted to go. My parole came when I saw my do-in-order-to-be orientation for what it really was. I knew that freedom involved stepping out beyond myself and what I could control, stepping into an unknown future.

To do so required faith, real faith, not some intellectually based, religious game. I needed to actively trust in something beyond myself. I realized how ironic it was that fulfilling the longing to find myself was ultimately not about me and what I brought to the table.

There's a Chinese proverb that says, "When the student is ready, the teacher arrives."

Finally, I was ready for the Teacher.

DISAMBIGUATION
CHAPTER 3

THE BIG IDEA:

We–ourselves–are the biggest barrier to finding our true identity. The identity we long for is beyond our ability to create, so we must go beyond ourselves to find it.

NOT KNOWING HOW TO FIND IDENTITY IS A PROBLEM.

We end up wasting time, running in circles and getting nowhere.[13]

WE SEARCH FOR IDENTITY LIKE WE'RE CONSUMERS.

Discovering who we want to be is a longing, but we approach it as if it were a craving–expecting a quick fix on *our* terms, where *we're* in control. We view God as the great Spiritual Service Provider who should give us what we think we need when we think we need it.[14]

OUR CONSCIENCE IS A MORAL WAYFINDER FOR IDENTITY.

It judges our actions, motives and thoughts. Our conscience is clear when our life and identity are aligned, and it's conflicted when they aren't. If we listen to our conscience, it will be our guide, and if we don't, it becomes calloused and silent. God created it in us, it's the hidden compass in our being that points to him.[15]

WE ARE THE FISHBOWL WE LIVE IN.

We are the barrier to discovering our own identity. We are the reason we can't discover who we are or see who we want to be. Moving beyond ourselves, by definition, is a step of faith. Since we don't know what we'll find, we can't depend on anything we currently possess, and no one else can take our steps of faith for us.[16]

PART 2

Starting Over

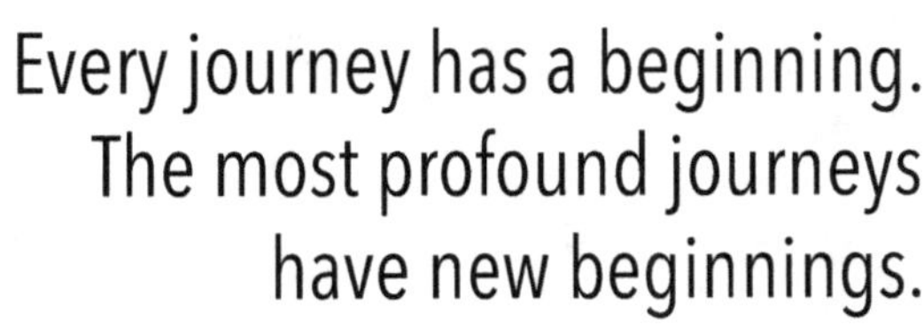

Every journey has a beginning.
The most profound journeys
have new beginnings.

Chapter Four

Of Beggars, Mourners and Meekers

What lens are you looking through to see yourself?

IT WAS PREDAWN, no longer night and not yet day, and a little crisp by Florida standards. The buildings to the east were backlit with an orange haze. I pulled off Fourth Street into the parking lot, suddenly waking to the realization that I was the only car on the road. In a few hours, Fourth Street would be the backstretch in the race for the high life. But at the moment, I could have crossed the street to Shep's Deli without bothering to look.

The office of the church I worked for at the time was in a converted 40s bungalow. "That office has good karma," a former tenant once described it. "I liked the hardwood floors the best. It's homey, and Fourth Street has such a cool vibe. It's the perfect office."

It was on Fourth Street, almost literally. From the curb, there was a small easement, then the sidewalk, then the elevated and covered front porch that ran the full width of the former house. It was so close to the street that when fire trucks made their run with sirens blaring, the conversation usually had to pause. It all added to the reality of being "on Fourth Street."

I was going up the three steps onto the porch when I sensed something, a dark shape, hiding in the corner's deep shadow. As my focus adjusted, I realized it was a living shape, curled up under a well-worn blanket, snoring. My nose concurred with my eyes as I picked up the scent of someone who had not showered in many days.

The scent of the street.

I stepped past him to the door, which I tried to open as quietly as possible—unsuccessfully. Startled and confused, he looked up at me and deadpanned, "I was sleeping."

I wasn't sure if he was apologizing or griping. Not knowing what to say, I settled on the first thing that came to mind, "Yeah, you were."

We gazed at each other through the predawn dimness. Finally, I broke the silence.

"Look, you can go back to sleep, but you can't stay here. This isn't a place to call home."

He looked relieved, although the thought of finding tomorrow's home seemed to weigh on him. He nodded a curt affirmation and slipped his head back under the blanket.

I turned and went into the office, locking the door behind me.

What was that all about?

I moved to Florida in 2001 from the 'burbs of Chicago. My move included a nasty divorce. I was leaving her and frankly couldn't care less about it. She had nagged me for the last four years, and I just couldn't take it anymore. She could find someone else to bother now. I left her all alone, leaning against the wall in the empty garage. I don't even know if she was crying because I never looked back. I simply didn't need her anymore. I was shedding no tears over deserting my partner for the last four winters, my snow shovel.

Cheryl and I moved to St. Pete with our kids just a few weeks before Thanksgiving. Shortly after we arrived, we decided to drive around town to get a lay of the land. We stopped at a light and saw a couple in the crosswalk. Arm-in-arm, they clutched each other as they walked, pooling their body heat to stave off the beast of winter. They were decked out in full winter gear—gloves, winter coats … even earmuffs. I glanced at Cheryl, the perplexed look on her face mirroring my own. I looked at the car's thermometer, which read 54 degrees, then glanced at my jeans and denim shirt with rolled-up sleeves.

Wow … we're not in Chicago anymore.

Since we arrived in 2001, we've yet to have a winter below 32 degrees. One of the realities of this subtropical climate is that it's easier on the homeless. They're not everywhere, but they're easy to see if you look for them. They walk the streets, contrasting sharply with the high-rise condos and sailboats, waterfront homes and BMW convertibles. They live slowly and deliberately for today, while the world around them lives fast and furious for tomorrow. It's a curious juxtaposition, the homeless amidst the high life.

It's a curious juxtaposition, the homeless amidst the high life.

Jeanne wasn't a homeless person. Far from it, in fact.

She was an accomplished neuromuscular massage therapist. Her daughter was in our kid's carpool, so we often learned of her travels to the East Coast, or Denver or Japan. Once, she consulted with a surgical team who had separated twins born conjoined at the head. When she wasn't traveling, she was training other therapists or working with the Tampa Bay Rays training staff, using massage techniques to help the Rays win the American League pennant. When she wasn't busy with this, she was writing her second textbook.

Jeanne effectively juggled single parenthood with everything else. She was always prompt, intensely yet pleasantly so. She was keen on details of school and schedules and days to pick up. She was always on top of things.

That is, until the day she wasn't.

"I got some bad news from the doctor," she said one day, out of earshot of her daughter. "I've been through a battery of tests, and …" she began streaming medicalese that quickly revealed the gaps in my knowledge of the female anatomy.

"Anyway, I need to have immediate surgery. The doctor says there are two possible outcomes. One is waking up with a few parts missing," she said with a tense smile and a light-hearted twitch of her head. But then her smile faded, and reality hit her right in the countenance.

"The other is waking up with a few months left to live."

What do you say in times like this? The fact that there wasn't a seminary course on how to deal with these situations confronted me once again, as it so often had in the past. I'm not sure what I said next, probably something profound like, "Whoa," or "Man."

"But I'm ok," she added. "In fact, I actually feel … at peace."

Over the previous months, we'd had a number of discussions about faith and spirituality. Jeanne grew up in a church that talked about Jesus, but it was a Jesus who held a sword in one hand and a judge's gavel in the other.

I can honestly say I'm more at peace now than when I was in control.

"I don't go to church anymore," she admitted. "But I've never lost my faith. I still pray, I still read the Bible. I still believe."

"So tell me, why this sense of peace?"

"Well, it's strange. At first there was so much to do, including talk with the surgeon, battle with the insurance company, update my will … But then, there was nothing else to do, nothing else I *could* do. That really made me anxious because that's unfamiliar territory for me. But then I realized it's all up to God now."

Sobered by her own reflection, she said, "I guess I'm at a place where I really have no choice but to trust God completely. The only true prayer I have left is 'Thy will be done.' So that's what I'm praying. It's changed me—it really has. I can honestly say I'm more at peace now than when I was in control."

What's up with that?

"Dad, there's a man at the front door," my daughter Hannah announced one Saturday morning. As she darted off, she added, "He looks kind of weird."

I opened the door to an aged, bent, black man whose life had not been kind to him. He was weathered and thin and held a rake that looked as worn as he did.

"Hi, can I help you?"

"I's wondrin' if you had any yard work you needed doin'." His speech was slurred, his words running together.

"I got an apartment over here, with a roommate. Between the two of us, we can just about cover the rent. But I need to work to buy bread and some other groceries. I can't get a job because I had a stroke a few years back, and no one'll hire me. So I just go around the neighborhood and ask people if they have any yard work they need done. Most people just call me the Yard Man."

His teeth were gapped, colored and worn, like dried kernels on an old corn cob. Many were missing. His eyes were cataracted and bloodshot, and one seemed to drift off target. It was hard to know which one to look at.

"Well, I'm trying to get my sons to do the yard work," I countered.

"I'll work hard, and I won't be any trouble. I could do some of the raking for you, pick up some of these leaves or palm fronds."

Embarrassed, I said, "Sorry, not today. I'm gonna get my boys on it."

Disappointed that I was turning down ready help, he looked away. "Okay. I'm not trying to be a bother or scare anyone. I respect women, and I seen your wife and daughter. I respect women," he repeated as he turned to leave.

"Thanks, I appreciate that. Maybe some other time, though," I offered.

"All right now, have a nice day," he slurred over his shoulder as he ambled away, the effects of the stroke evident in his stride.

He took my offer of "maybe another time" seriously. He passed by on many Saturdays and sometimes during the week. Over time we let him do some work, which he did quietly and faithfully. He asked for a bit of money each time, never too much and never without working for it.

We finally learned his real name was James. We gave him food every now and then, although, with his teeth, we learned to offer bananas instead of apples.

"I just need enough money to pay for the pain medicine for my teeth," he slurred one day. That's the way it always was, a little bit of money to cover something for that week.

He sat with Cheryl on our back porch once, eating some of our leftover spaghetti. He told her of how he had come to know Jesus as he was recovering from alcohol addiction. He had done so many things he regretted. "But Jesus saved me, and I know he's gonna' take care of me. That's all I need to know."

Then one day, he was gone. He never came round again. "I guess he's with Jesus now," Cheryl mused. As we talked about him, it struck me that I'm not sure I've ever met a more contented person.

What's that all about?

It's a cold slap in the face to realize that Jesus—the champion of my faith, the Savior of my soul and my example to follow—was a homeless man.

He lived on the street, sleeping wherever he could, wherever he should. "Foxes have holes and birds have nests, but the Son of Man has no place to lay his head," he once claimed. "A man of no reputation," Rich Mullins sang of him.

I wonder if he had the scent of the street about him.

Maybe that's part of the reason the religious elite despised him. He claimed, of all things, to be the Messiah—God's Chosen One, prophesied to redeem and liberate God's people. But he didn't fit the part. No Messiah they'd ever conceived looked, talked or ... smelled like him. His greatest distinction was what he lacked.

I think of the Bible story of Simon the Pharisee inviting Jesus over for a meal. As a Pharisee, Simon was part of the political/religious social leadership of Jesus' day, the clergy who ran the government. Given his position, Simon was taking a bit of a risk having this controversial, homeless rabbi at his dinner table.

Simon's hospitality was perfunctory and minimal. He didn't offer any water for Jesus to wash his feet. He didn't even offer a kiss of welcome, the Jewish equivalent of a hearty handshake.

Things really got weird, though, when *she* came in. *She* was "a sinner," likely a known prostitute with a disregard for Jewish social and religious customs. She began pouring expensive, perfumed oil on Jesus' feet. She mingled it with her tears, an eruption of sorrow and regret mixed with forgiveness and joy. I wonder what Simon was thinking. *Now what? How inconsiderate! Who does she think she is?*

The woman with the bad reputation threw off all restraint and washed and kissed the feet of a homeless man whose hand Simon, the Pharisee of esteemed reputation, wouldn't even shake. The contrast couldn't be sharper.

If Jesus were a homeless man sitting on my front porch, I doubt I'd recognize him.

It's easy to get down on Simon. I read the story through the sanitized lenses of modern faith, where our hero Jesus is as obviously God as the haloed pictures we've made of him. But Simon didn't see a halo or smell the incense of heaven. Simon saw a homeless, itinerant, trouble-making preacher from the backwoods of Nowheresville. He smelled the scent of the street.

I'm forced to ask myself which character I am, Simon or the woman. The answer undoes me. If Jesus were a homeless man sitting on my front porch, I doubt I'd recognize him. "I've been waiting to talk," he would say. But I'd probably hear it as a gripe, not a request to come in.

"Yeah, you have," I'd likely respond, hoping he'd get my point and remove himself. I'd probably step right by him, closing and locking the door behind me.

What's that all about?

The gospel of Matthew tells of another encounter between Jesus and a clergyman, a teacher of the Law. Being one rung down from a Pharisee, he might even be considered well-to-do. He is comfortable in his role and ministry, with an established reputation.

"I will follow you wherever you go," he boldly claimed to Jesus. For the clergyman, there was something exciting about Jesus. He sensed a new calling for himself, a new way to leverage his experience and knowledge. Maybe this is the opportunity he's been yearning for.

"Foxes have holes," Jesus replied, knowing the choice this man faces. "And birds of the air have nests, but the Son of Man has no place to lay his head."

Reading between the lines, I strain to see the man's response. Will he embrace the new identification with Jesus or pause to weigh his options? Will he value God over the brand he was building for himself? The tension mounts as I will him to move forward, to surrender his old identity with all its trappings.

But he hesitates, his shoulders slump and his spirit falls under the weight of his choice. His sadness becomes mine. As I look closer into the man's face, I can see a familiar confusion in his eyes.

That man is me!

Left unchecked, I will spin my wheels in the fast and furious race for the relevant life. I will push and yank in the scrum of the beautiful life. I will toil, crafting a reputable identity that I can surf like a wave. I *believe* I should *be somebody*. I rely on myself, on what I've done and what I believe I will do. I pursue social acceptance, esteem and accomplishment in order to make something of myself.

The chase for this false identity is so powerful that it changes the way I see Jesus. I conform him into a superhero. I shower off the street scent, put him in hip clothes and hand him an iPhone. I create a sanitized Jesus, a relevant Jesus that matches the false identity of who I want to be.

My beautiful Jesus doesn't smell like the street. He's humble when he needs to be, in spin and sound bites. My beautiful Jesus has marketable humility, like a political candidate for a photo op in a soup kitchen. He's the Christian CEO, sitting on a donkey to get his message across.

I like this sanitized, cleaned-up Jesus. It's easy to follow *that* Jesus. I could almost be like *that* Jesus.

The only problem is that my beautiful Jesus isn't Jesus.

"Blessed are the poor in spirit," Jesus once said. The spiritually bankrupt. The beggars with no spiritual capital or bartering currency. No reputation or religious portfolio to exchange for God's blessing. Nothing to rely on except God's goodness and grace. No prayer beyond Jeanne's prayer of "Thy will be done."

"Blessed are those who mourn, for they will be comforted. Blessed are the meek, for they will inherit the earth." Blessed are the beggars, the mourners and the meekers. Not because they beg or mourn or act meekly. They're blessed because they see beyond the fleeting, temporal things of this world to a time and place where truth, peace and justice will hold the day. That's who they will be, and so that's who they are now. That's their ethos, who they want to be.

Only a homeless Jesus could promote a spirituality and identity not made of this world.

Only a homeless Jesus—someone who set aside the scent of heaven and replaced it with the scent of the street—could make that claim with integrity and power. Only a homeless Jesus could promote a spirituality and identity not made of this world. Only he could show that our world—with all its fast and furious pursuits of the relevant life—is not a place to call home. Only this Jesus could invite me to join him by abandoning a hollow, shallow approach that lusts for self-reliance and public standing.

He invites me to go the way of humility rather than the way of pride. Pride, after all, caused the greatest identity change in all of creation, as Lucifer, the original angel of light, looked at himself in the mirror and thought, "Hmmm, I'm really something … " Pride caused Adam and Eve to buy into the lie that they could be like God—when they were already like God in every way that mattered. Pride dogs me to hold on to a worthless, Outside-In approach that's only momentarily relevant.

Pride is what got us into this mess. Why in the world do we think pride can help us get out of it?

The choice is mine. Will I embrace the new identification with Jesus or pause to weigh my options? The tension mounts as I will myself to move forward, to surrender my old identity with all its collateral. Can I accept that, in God's economy, a sinful woman with nothing to offer is held in higher esteem than a credentialed Pharisee? Could I let go of everything I've ever pursued and all the trappings that go with it—my pursuit of, and belief, in my elaborate approach to life—to be a beggar, a mourner and a meeker?

Can I accept that, in God's economy, a sinful woman with nothing to offer is held in higher esteem than a credentialed Pharisee?

The irony of it all is that this homeless Jesus wants my heart for his home. "Behold, I stand at the door and knock," Jesus says.

"I'm on your front porch," he says to me once again.

"Yeah, you are," I say back to him.

What do I do with a homeless Jesus on my front porch?

DISAMBIGUATION
CHAPTER 4

THE BIG IDEA:

We can't be who we want to be on our own,
or through chasing what the world offers as significant.

WE NATURALLY PURSUE IDENTITIES THAT ALIGN WITH THINGS LIKE RELEVANCE, POWER, INFLUENCE, STATUS AND ACCUMULATION.

These are qualities that society promotes and celebrates, the metrics for existential significance. They're also what our flesh craves (see Chapter 1), which is a powerful combination to resist.[17]

WE ALSO SHUN IDENTITIES OF WEAKNESS, INSIGNIFICANCE AND MODESTY.

Because we view neediness or indigence negatively, we detach from certain people or lifestyles because we don't want the association to reflect negatively on us.[18]

AN IDENTITY OF CONTROL GIVES US A FALSE SENSE OF SOVEREIGNTY.

There's actually very little in this life that we can truly control. We should plan and be wise. But to operate as if we are in total control of our lives is to live in deception.[19]

THE IDENTITY WE SEEK CANNOT BE FOUND THROUGH PUBLIC APPROVAL, STUFF OR STATUS.

They are zeroes in the identity equation. Knowing this frees us from the burden of pursuing them as a way to be valued and relevant and lets us clearly see the gap between who we are and who we want to be.[20]

WE MUST ABANDON PRIDE.

Pride is keeping an inordinately high view of self. By definition, it is a false identity. Pride is at the root of chasing after relevance, power, influence, status and accumulation. It was the catalyst for the fall of humankind–the reason we're on this identity search to begin with. We cannot find our true, created identity using the same approach that brought about its loss.[21]

JESUS' IDENTITY WAS NOT OF THIS WORLD.

Relevance in this world meant nothing to him. He came from heaven, after all, he was just visiting here.[22]

WE CANNOT KNOW WHO WE WANT TO BE UNTIL WE LIBERATE OURSELVES FROM THE IDENTITY THE WORLD DRIVES US TOWARD.

It's possible to be meek and poor in spirit and also be relevant and significant. Jesus was, and he changed the world forever. There is a way to detach ourselves from the things that feed an identity of self-reliance and self-importance, but it must be chosen.[23]

Chapter Five

Thirsty

How do you deal with the awareness that you're not yet a "finished product?"

One summer, I installed a sprinkler system. Why I chose to do it in August—the peak of summer in Florida—is still a mystery. I also had a friend, Doug, who was willing to help. He was thinking about putting a system in his yard, and we agreed to swap and help each other.

Come to think of it, Doug moved out of state not long after that. Hmmm.

On the surface, Florida summers don't appear that bad when you only look at the average high temperature of 91 degrees. But the average humidity in the summer is 72 percent. It doesn't get over 91 because it can't, the air is too saturated. As the temperature rises, it doesn't get hotter. It gets steamier.

Walking in the heat of a summer day feels more like wading. Your glasses fog when you walk out of an air-conditioned building. Sweat doesn't evaporate, it clings. There's no way around it, it's just hot.

About halfway through the sprinkler system project, I became aware of a desperate thirst at a level I'd never felt before. Despite constantly drinking fluids, I never felt hydrated. It was insatiable, and even days after the work was done, I found myself drinking more than usual.

It brought up a morbid thought. What would happen if my body's thirst response were somehow turned off? I doubt I'd drink water. I don't particularly like the taste of water. I think if I couldn't sense thirst, I'd die of dehydration, even with water available at the tap just a few feet away.

Though still thirsty, I came to appreciate the mechanism of thirst. It is my body's way of telling me what it needs, reminding me that drinking deeply gives life. We often think that something's wrong if we're needy. But thirst makes me intentional, it forces me to look for the things that truly quench.

As David Wilcox sings, "All the roots go deeper when it's dry."

I remember walking toward campus for my first class in seminary. *You're getting one of the best Bible education in the world. You're going to be prepared for ministry. You'll know everything you need to know, so you'll be able to help others.*

The seminary was where the really mature Christians went, the hall of champions. It was like Oz, where Dorothy and her friends could get what they needed most. It was where people lived their lives around the castle of the knowledge of God. Oz was a destination, and I believed graduating there would bring a sense that I'd arrived from a spiritual perspective. I looked forward to the day I'd be done and wouldn't have to grow anymore.

Looking back on it now, it was like saying I expected to map out the edge of the universe or confirm the chemical composition of love.

I looked forward to the day I'd be done and wouldn't have to grow anymore.

I remember walking across the stage to get my diploma after four of the most difficult years I've ever lived. *Finally! But … why does this feel more like a beginning than an end? Why do I have more questions now than when I started? Lord, I need a job!*

I graduated from Oz knowing less than I knew when I started. Don't get me wrong, it was a wonderful learning experience and an outstanding preparation for my future. In fact, it was probably just the education I needed. But seminary didn't decode the genome of the knowledge of God. Instead, it revealed whole new worlds of things I didn't know—and couldn't know—about him.

It didn't do much for my self-confidence. On paper, it was hard to justify investing my entire life savings and all the hours of study to learn how much I didn't know. Adding insult to injury, people weren't particularly impressed with my seminary degree. Having my diploma hanging on my wall didn't motivate them to follow my lead.

I know, naïve, right? Looking back, I didn't really believe I'd know it all and that people would follow me blindly. But that's what I *wanted*. I'm embarrassed to talk about it, except that it's true. And I know, on some level, it's true for so many others.

We live so many parts of our lives in a fantasy, an Oz-like expectation of being finished and complete. Whether it's jobs, relationships, reputations … whatever, we pursue the stuff of life with the goal of being full.

And when we're full, we won't have to worry about being empty—we won't need anything from anyone. We won't have to trust anyone else to give us something we don't have. We want to arrive. Because once we've arrived, we'll no longer be sojourners.

We have a bias for arrival.

I noticed something the other day—a sponge.

I picked it up and immediately realized it was soaking wet, full of water. It was much heavier than I expected. It was so saturated, in fact, that it left a puddle on the counter where it sat.

I had a spill to clean, but before I could use the sponge, I had to wring it out. After wringing it out, I immediately picked up the scent of mildew, not only from the sponge but now also from my hand, which I felt compelled to wash with soap. I got out a clean cloth to take care of the spill and threw the sponge away.

For a sponge to work right, it needs to be thirsty. A saturated sponge soaks up nothing else, nothing new. It leaves a mess wherever it goes.

And after a while, it stinks.

For many years, Cheryl and I and our three young kids traveled from Florida to Arkansas to be with my mom and siblings for Thanksgiving. But the first Thanksgiving after mom died, we stayed in Florida. Although we missed being with our extended family, it turned out to be one of the most enjoyable Thanksgivings we've ever had.

A saturated sponge soaks up nothing else, nothing new. It leaves a mess wherever it goes.

Maybe it was one of those years when I just needed the time off. Maybe it was the chance to spend two days relaxing instead of driving. Whatever it was, I wish I could bottle it.

The kids and I put all the dishes together the day before Thanksgiving. Everyone pitched in to make the cheesy potatoes, the sweet potatoes, the pies and the salads. We slept late, put it all in the oven along with the ham, ate when it was done and then dozed in front of a movie until it was time for seconds.

Now that's what I call a holiday!

There were two parts to the meal—anticipation and participation.

First, the anticipation.

We planned the meal together. We talked about it days in advance, thinking about how good it was going to be and how right it was for Cheryl to just show up and eat (instead of bearing her usual burden of meal prep). We picked each person's favorite dish and eliminated what he or she didn't want. You know how sometimes you have to eat Great Grandma's traditional fruit bread so she won't be offended? Not today.

We anticipated as we made the meal together. Rolling out the piecrusts. Cutting up the fruit. Boiling the sweet potatoes. Chopping the onions and bell pepper for the squash casserole while the pumpkin and apple pies are baking. The smells filled the house for the rest of the day. It all confirmed that something extraordinary was coming.

Life is lived on a deeper level when you are looking forward to something intently. Kids, anticipating Christmas for weeks, burst out of their beds on Christmas morning to see what's under the tree. The weak-kneed groom strains to see his bride turn the corner and walk down the aisle and into his life, the vision he's been dreaming about for months.

The anticipation is half the fun.

Then came the participation. The hours of drawing in the smells of Thanksgiving made for sensory overload when we finally partook together. The ham was just as I expected, salty and honey and juicy. The strawberry Jell-O salad, tart and sweet. Every bite was better than the one before. And the pecan pie was so rich that my mouth still waters at the thought of it.

It truly was a day of Thanksgiving. We laughed. We told stories. We recalled memories from the past years. We talked about the things we were grateful for. At one point, we all became aware of the shared satisfaction of a communal meal, where we shared in each other's satisfaction. We consumed each other's laughter and enjoyment, coming away happier and more contented than we ever could have been on our own.

It was a genuine celebration, even with dirty pots and pans.

I've pushed back from the table after many a meal with the sensation of being full. Truth be told, my approach to most meals is to be filled. There's no anticipation, no preparation apart from the routine necessity of coming up with something to eat. I'm motivated by hunger, I don't want to be hungry anymore. So I consume, get 'er done and move on.

Most of these meals are unremarkable. Even though the food may be tasty and nutritious, the meals don't warrant remembering. I realize that not every meal can be Thanksgiving. But compared to the everyday meals, I find it profound that Thanksgiving is such an experience.

There's a difference between wanting to get rid of your hunger and hungering for ultimate satisfaction.

One comes from the stomach, the other from the heart.

I heard the other day that the economy is changing the way we shop.

"In a down economy, people look for more value," the TV news reporter chimed. "One store understands that, and their business is booming this Christmas."

She then spent the next few minutes profiling a consignment store for high-dollar accessory items. They had a great deal on Gucci purses that originally sold for $400, now a steal at $90. Because times were tight, purse shoppers let go of their reservations about buying pre-owned.

She went on to talk about how the economy was affecting attitudes about Christmas shopping. Multiple interviews portrayed shoppers who felt good about spending less, like one man who bought a $40 pair of shoes instead of the $80 pair. They weren't necessarily happy, but they were content—like it was the right thing to do.

Personally, I have a hard time getting my mind around $90 for a purse, much less $400. Granted, I don't carry a purse, so maybe if I did, I'd feel differently. But having gone through some lean financial years, I view $90 much differently now. I think in terms of how far Cheryl can stretch $90 at the supermarket. $90 would pay half of my summer electric bill.

When I'm financially thirsty, I tend to focus on stuff I need instead of stuff I use.

But there's a bigger issue in play here, something beyond the practicalities of managing income. For instance, people who earn less give 30 percent more of their income to charities—*30 percent!* Why is it that people with less money give more of it away?

Is it the realization that money isn't what it's cracked up to be?

Does living in need allow you to relate to *someone else's* needs?

And what is it about *not* being in need that changes us?

A quick internet search will confirm that wealthy people, as a whole, are more stressed, insecure, anxious, depressed, guilty, vulnerable, self-conscious, concerned about appearances and afraid. Curiously, much of the fear comes from focusing on what they don't have. One article quoted an expert who works with high-net-worth people. "They never do feel they have enough. It takes some coaxing to get them to spend money."[24]

What is it about *not* being in need that changes us?

Another article revealed how the wealthy tend to compare themselves with those who have more wealth (instead of those who have less). They see themselves and their spending habits as normal and middle-class. One example was Helen, a stay-at-home mom with a household income of $2 million and assets of $8 million. "They have private planes," she said of the wealthy. "They have drivers. They have all these things … Money makes everything easier … And, you know, we don't have that luxury in that way.'"[25]

I would think most people would jump at the chance to have a net worth north of $10 million. But are we prepared for the way it would change how we see ourselves? Another expert observed that "There's this undercurrent that money equals love, power, security, control, self-worth, self-love, freedom, self-esteem—all those loaded things that money supposedly can do, but doesn't."[26]

Instead of providing peace, confidence and contentment, wealth can actually steal them. Instead of clarifying and simplifying life, it complicates and confuses it. It can create an artificial reality, removing our awareness of thirst.

And when we're not thirsty, we don't drink deeply.

In the first year of our marriage, I had the opportunity to take a one-year offsite assignment at my engineering job. Cheryl and I packed up and moved to the high desert north of Los Angeles. The drive across the stark desert Southwest in July was unforgettable. Growing up in the hills and lakes of Arkansas didn't prepare me for the experience of breathing in 120-degree air at 10 percent humidity.

We stopped at Joshua Tree National Park to see the park's namesake. *Yucca Brevifolia* is part of the agave family and is one of the more unique trees in the world. Legend has it that Mormon settlers traveling west named the tree after the biblical story of Joshua holding his arms up while the Israelites battled against their enemies. The name makes sense when you see the tree in person.

When it's dry, your roots need to go deep.

It's amazing that any plant can survive the harsh conditions in the desert, let alone thrive and grow to 49 feet as the tallest ones have. But it's not as surprising when you consider that the trees have a strong and extensive root system, some reaching as deep as 36 feet—virtually as tall underground as it is above ground.

When it's dry, your roots need to go deep. It's the only way to thrive in a world that offers you nothing to quench your thirst.

As I said earlier, I enjoy a good hot dog. We don't eat them much anymore, but when the kids were young, hot dogs were an easy, go-to meal solution. I'm holding out hope that someone will discover a healthy link to eating hot dogs. I hold out some hope, but not much. A hot dog is what it is, and it ain't what it ain't.

The first few bites of a dog are satisfying. It's a meal made for the right moment, whether at a game, from the downtown street vendor between buildings and lunch and dinner, or outside Lowes when you've made your second trip to get the parts you forgot on the first one. The smell of a cooking dog in the open air is hard to resist.

But I confess my enjoyment of hot dogs has become a love-hate thing. After the moment it takes to eat a hot dog, it's gone. And in another moment, a second dog. And if I'm feeling really manly, a third. After I'm done, I get a strange sensation of fullness. The sensations at the end of the hot dog meal don't match up to the expectations at the beginning.

If you Google "hot dog eating," you'll eventually find a photo of Joey Chestnut, who, as of this writing, is currently ranked first in the world by Major League Eating. In one image I saw, he apparently just ate the winning hot dog. His right hand is raised with a victory fist, and his left hand is covering his mouth. There's a pained look on his face, and his eyes are squinched. It's not clear whether he's stuffing the dog in or he's trying to keep it from coming back out.

Joey, call sign "Jaws," has multiple world championships to his credit. At the 2020 Nathan's Hot Dog Eating Contest (fittingly held on the Fourth of July), he set a new record by consuming 75 hot dogs and buns in 10 minutes. The next closest competitor downed 42 dogs (what a wimp!). In 2021, Joey upped his game to a new world record of 76—one hot dog every eight seconds.

Wow, 76 hot dogs … makes me feel pretty good about stopping at three. I wonder how these guys feel the next day. What happens to you after eating 76 of those things?

I wonder why that never made the news …

Though I can't imagine eating 76, I can tell you that after eating three, the appeal is gone. The smell turns from "gourmet" to "gotcha," and the burp that's coming next is not very satisfying either.

I got what I craved. Now I'm heavy and bloated, with a twinge of regret mixed in.

I am full.

There are some restaurants that I truly enjoy. One is Bonefish Grill, which Chris Parker and some friends started as a local spot in St. Pete. They converted an old sports bar on Fourth Street with a vision for a great fish place that served exceptional food with even better service.

Their vision became a reality. Bonefish went big and eventually became part of a corporate brand. It's a place where you feel honored and appreciated from the moment you walk in the door. I usually have a great experience there.

Which is saying something because I really don't like fish.

It's common for my last bite at Bonefish to taste as good (if not better than) the first. Sometimes I stop eating, not because I'm full, but because I'm satisfied. I could eat more, it's not like I'm stuffed. I simply realize I didn't need to eat anymore. Eating at Bonefish is not about being full, it's being satisfied.

Experiences like Bonefish tell me life is best when we're a little bit hungry, a little bit thirsty. We can actually be more fulfilled, achieve more, have greater influence and be more disciplined when we stay on the thirsty side of life. There are examples all around us, after all. People who stay curious learn more. People who fail innovate more (though it's probably more accurate to say innovators fail more since some people who fail just stop). People who earn less give more. Sports teams, perhaps less talented but "hungry" to win, often beat teams of superior athletes.

Life is best when we're a little bit hungry, a little bit thirsty.

Life's better when we stay thirsty, but part of me won't embrace this idea because being thirsty feels somehow … incomplete. My old identity is afraid of lacking, so it pushes me to arrive and get it all together. And it enjoys the boost to its pride when I get to promote my arrival.

Of course, this part of me won't admit to pride. Instead, I occasionally throw out quippy, self-defacing comments as a way to save face, a spin of false humility on what I hope looks like the image of someone who's arrived.

The real question is more straight-up and all-in. Am I comfortable with an identity of hunger? Can I find significance, meaning and contentment in seeing myself—and having others see me—as one who is not yet full? Can I embrace the startling reality that my own self-determination can't satiate what I'm most thirsty for?

Will I shed my bias for arrival?

I'm confronted by Jesus' promise, "Blessed are those who hunger and thirst for righteousness, for they shall be satisfied."

It's easy to read this as some kind of nirvanic promise that someday, I won't hunger or thirst ever again. Yet I can't help but wonder: Isn't it also a promise that I can be satisfied today, right here and now?

In our compulsion to be filled, we can misinterpret the sensations of hunger and thirst. They aren't there just to tell us when we're full. They are there to drive us toward real nutrition. They remind us that drinking deeply goes way beyond just wetting the throat. It gives life.

Hungering and thirsting for all things to be made right is our soul's way of telling us what it needs most. The thirst reminds us that life comes through drinking deeply, of living water. If we turn off our spiritual and existential thirst response, we'll die of dehydration with the cure sitting right in front of us.

Thanksgivings and hot dogs and Bonefish remind me that hunger and thirst point to satisfaction, which I then strive to find—roots growing deeper when it's dry.

It all hinges on the question of who I aspire to be. Do I want to be the person chasing after fullness and arrival, with all their empty promises, false notoriety and perceived stability? Or, rather, do I want to be the person content to live with daily longings for what God wants to provide for me?

I remember one time when I was visiting friends in France, and some of their friends invited me over for dinner. That they didn't speak much English and I didn't speak any French made it interesting. Actually, I knew "hello" and "croissant," and I could count to ten. That got me through the first minute. So for the rest of the evening, it was gestures and putting sentences together from my pocket French-English dictionary.

It was one of the most enjoyable meals I've ever had. Salad. Cheese. Bread. Appetizer. Main course. First dessert, then a second dessert. Coffee. It lasted for three hours. The food was amazing. The hospitality was warm and wonderful. We laughed, though we couldn't understand each other very well. It's funny how you can bond with people at a level deeper than language.

I left their apartment satisfied in ways I can't explain, on levels I didn't even know existed. I'd heard that meals in France are righteous events, and I experienced it firsthand. You can eat well in France, but it's not just about the food. It's about being together and the pleasure of eating delicious food prepared as a celebration. It's the right thing, the right way to take care of hunger.

Our deep longings are evidence. They wouldn't be there unless there was a way to fulfill them.

The invitation to be content with hunger and thirst in the present sounds foolish unless it's tied to the promise of ultimate satisfaction coming in the future. The promise forces us into a decision. We can dismiss this idea of ultimate satisfaction as wishful thinking and be left with our present hunger. Or we can believe in a future satisfaction because we know—in ways we can't explain and at levels we're not sure even exist—that it's coming. Our deep longings are evidence. They wouldn't be there unless there was a way to fulfill them, a way that's just as deep, just as profound, just as real.

I find it compelling that Jesus would describe heaven as a feast, the Great Banquet. All who respond to the invitation are gathered there. They've been anticipating this day for so long. People are there from all over. Their kinship goes deeper than language, bonded on a level more significant and personal than words can express. And hey, a bonus, there are no pots and pans to clean!

The hospitality is rich, the joy flowing, and the food … well, it's not about the food, is it?

It's righteous.

It's the right way to take care of hunger.

DISAMBIGUATION
CHAPTER 5

THE BIG IDEA:

It's better to acknowledge that we'll always be lacking in this life, so we'll pursue the things that make us right and complete (and stop fixating on the things that don't).

YOU DRINK MORE WHEN YOU'RE THIRSTY.

We tend to think that lacking anything is bad and wrong, a position of weakness and low standing. That's actually greed and pride doing their work. Status and accumulation become our gods, our idols. We accredit them with superpowers, then trust them to remove our lacking.

But they can't. The best they can do is disguise and distract. If we're conscious of what we lack, we'll look for the only thing that can satisfy our deepest thirst.[27]

WE'RE NATURALLY BIASED TOWARD ARRIVAL.

We tend to live with the expectation that we'll arrive at a finish line where we won't have to learn anymore, be surprised, work, or have to change or adapt. Crossing this line means we won't have to trust or have faith anymore, we'll be in control.[28]

IT'S DANGEROUS TO STOP LEARNING, GROWING AND ADAPTING.

The moment we think we've arrived is the moment we stop living. We're actually lying to ourselves, saying we've arrived when we know we haven't. It's easy to become closed-minded, bitter, anxious, hypocritical, judgmental, cynical, self-righteous, divisive and isolated. No one really wants to spend much time with us, and we lose our opportunity for influence.[29]

ANTICIPATING A BETTER TOMORROW GIVES JOY AND HOPE FOR TODAY.

Knowing a better future is coming puts our present in a more appropriate context. The joys are just deposits of even greater joys to come, hardships are tempered by the knowledge that they're temporary. Without anticipation, we're left with despair.[30]

THERE'S A DIFFERENCE BETWEEN BEING FULL AND BEING SATISFIED.

The urge to be full (whether it's eating or anything else in life) is actually based on fear. At its core is the belief that consuming and acquiring beyond our needs will somehow give us what we lack. The alternative is satisfaction–even as we recognize our lacking. Satisfaction is a state of being that isn't dependent on how full or empty we are.[31]

LIVING CLOSER TO THE THIRST THRESHOLD KEEPS US REAL.

This is not promoting self-imposed asceticism or extreme poverty–which is just another Outside-In, activity-based attempt at self-righteousness. Rather, living closer to the thirst threshold is intentionally unhitching our identity from the pursuit of "stuff"–regardless of how much of it we happen to have or not have.[32]

GOD HAS PROMISED A GREAT SATISFACTION, ONE AS DEEP AND PROFOUND AS THE LONGINGS WE'RE CURRENTLY EXPERIENCING.

Nothing we can do in this world will satiate what we hunger and thirst for. That makes the promise of the ultimate satisfaction so compelling. It's beyond our circumstances and ability to resolve.[33]

Chapter Six

Rest in Peace

What are you willing to give up
to be who you want to be …
and what does giving it up look like?

CURTIS WAS AT the theater with his wife, Vivian, to see *Lone Survivor.* He became irritated at Chad, who was sitting in front of him and using his phone during the preview.

Chad, a 43-year-old Navy veteran, and his wife Nicole were on a date. Chad was texting his three-year-old daughter's daycare to check in on her. Curtis and Chad exchanged comments, which soon escalated into words. Chad, an imposing man, became aggressive and threw his bag of popcorn in Curtis' face. Curtis, a 71-year-old retired police captain who now feared for his life, pulled out the concealed gun he was carrying and shot Chad in the chest.

Curtis and Vivian had planned to meet their son, Matthew, at the theater. Fifteen minutes earlier, Curtis had texted Matthew (who was running late) to let Matthew know they were already in their seats. Matthew, a police officer himself, came into the theater and was walking up the aisle when the shot rang out. He arrived just in time to catch Chad as he was collapsing in the aisle. Matthew, administering first aid and trying to figure out what had happened, looked up to see a shocked look on his dad's face.

Chad, who had no life insurance, died as Matthew was trying to save him from the use of deadly force exerted by his own father, who'd spent his career keeping the peace.[34]

Bruce's last three years had been hard. He lost his six-figure engineering job. Then his dog died. His wife filed for divorce.

Bruce couldn't deal anymore, so he dressed up as Santa and went to a Christmas party at his former in-law's home. He shot his ex-wife and eight other people, then used a homemade flamethrower to torch the home, burning himself badly in the process. In his last desperate act, he drove to his brother's house and shot himself.

Bruce had no criminal record or history of violence. He was an usher at his church. People that knew him said he'd always been a mild-mannered guy. It seems he was mild-mannered on the outside, and then suddenly, he wasn't.[35]

Another town, another tragedy. This house was gutted. "It was intentionally set on fire," said a spokesman for the Fire Marshall's office. Fortunately, no one was home, so no lives were lost. At least no lives were lost *this* time.

The "house" was actually a trailer. John, the man who used to live there, hadn't been in the trailer for four years. He had spent those years in custody for allegedly raping and murdering nine-year-old Jessica.

John had allegedly gone through an unlocked door of Jessica's nearby trailer at 3:00 a.m., waking her with a warning, "Don't yell or nothing." He then took her to his trailer, where he raped her and locked her in a closet while he went to work the next day. After three days, he couldn't figure out what to do with her, so he double-bagged her and buried her alive right outside the trailer, covering up the hole with leaves.

The trailer sat there, vacant, for four years. Someone threw a cement block through the window once. But apart from that, it remained with its empty shell, a lingering icon for the feeling such a story leaves in your gut.

I guess someone finally had enough and set fire to the thing. It sounds fitting and final. But you can't cover up violence with a pile of leaves, and you can't get peace by burning down a trailer.

The empty hole in your gut is still there.[36]

I could go on with more accounts like these, but hopefully, you get the point, and I'm feeling nauseous.

The world—life—is just not a peaceful place.

What is peace?

I *think* I know what it is.

I remember asking my son, Ryan, when he was a teenager what came to his mind when he thought about peace.

"People not killing each other," he said in a "duh" tone.

He's right, I think. World peace. It's what beauty queens call for, what diplomats are trained for, what military vets long for and what Jesus died for. Which makes you wonder. If peace is so important to so many people, why don't we see more of it?

I saw peace in our dog, Molly, when she was living. We called her The Love Sponge because she soaked up all the love you could give her. She made you breathe a little deeper, and petting her became addictive. One time our friends Owen and Cindy were over. Cindy was talking about something and started petting Molly, who had ambled in to be a part of the group and gazed at Cindy with big brown "pet me" eyes.

If peace is so important to so many people, why don't we see more of it?

"Molly's my therapy," she finally admitted aloud after realizing she had forgotten what she was talking about.

I see peace in other places, too. Polar bears, for instance. Maybe it's just how they look, but in most of the images I've seen, they look like they're just enjoying life. I've seen videos of polar bears sliding across the ice in their stomachs or pictures of them lazing around like the Thomas Mangelsen print *Bad Boys of the Arctic*. They always look like they're ambling about, never in a hurry.

I see peace in the face of a sleeping child. I remember how powerful it was to watch our kids sleep when they were infants (when they finally went to sleep). Maybe it was just relief that their activity had finally stopped, but watching them sleep was mesmerizing.

Incidentally, why is it that adults don't sleep as peacefully as infants? Look at the way we talk about sleep. "I was out of it," "I crashed" or "I ran out of gas."

Now that I think about it, I haven't seen many adults who look peaceful when they're awake, either. Most of us look harried and pained, like we're carrying around a secret too terrible to mention. We wear it on our furrowed brows and in our eyes. The eyes always tell.

Whatever peace is, we don't have it. And you can see it in our eyes.

Several years ago, my right ear started ringing. It was high-pitched and annoying, like a boiling teakettle on steroids, like a dog whistle might sound if I were a dog. It was barely audible but piercing and inescapable. Then it developed a low-pitched rumble, like when you stand too long and too close to the speakers at a rock concert. It mixed in with the ambient sounds to make a soupy stew of noise that made it hard to hear people talk. It was the last thing I heard before I went to sleep, and it was the first thing I heard when I woke up.

It was exhausting.

I went to the doctor, who then sent me to an audiologist, who in turn did a hearing test.

"There are no signs of damage, and your test shows you have excellent hearing," the doctor finally told me. "My guess is that you have an inner ear infection."

Being a parent, ear infections were a familiar concept.

"Okay, so there's a fluid buildup? Should I take antibiotics?"

"No, this is an *inner* ear infection," she answered with a look that told me I had just demonstrated my ignorance. "You can't get to it unless you drill through your skull, and I don't think you want to do that. Also, it's viral, antibiotics won't help. Your own immune system has to deal with it."

"So, I should take vitamins? Drink more orange juice?" I countered.

Uh oh, that look again. That must have been another stupid question. "Well, better nutrition is always good, but I don't know how much it will help your ear. You may see your symptoms come and go. But you will probably have this for the rest of your life."

A few years after that, I started getting bouts of vertigo. Oy, there's never a convenient time for vertigo. Again, I went to the doctor to get a prescription for something to take it away. She sent me to an ENT, who sent me, again, to the audiologist for another hearing test and then to a neurologist, who also had me do an MRI.

I didn't like where this was going. I just wanted a pill.

I finally ended up at an audio neurologist. The diagnosis on the table was Ménière's Disease, a debilitating condition that destroys the lining of the inner ear canals. The trifecta of symptoms is ringing, hearing loss and vertigo. I now had all three, and it looked like I was on the threshold of the disease fully manifesting.

The only way to know for sure was to wait and see. If it played out, I could expect worsening and more aggressive symptoms that would prevent me from driving or functioning normally. I might finally adapt and learn to live with it, or I could have surgery to sever the nerve. Either way, I would lose both my hearing and the sense of balance in that ear.

"What can I do?" I asked after the news finally hit bottom in my gut.

"Well, you can reduce your salt intake, and we can give you some diuretics. But the biggest thing is to reduce your stress. Are you under any stress?"

I AM NOW! What do you mean, am I under any stress?!? I wanted to scream but realized how stupid that was. I guess, finally, I'd learned what a stupid question is.

Something has to change.

How do you get peace? How about the perfect vacation, a get-away-from-it-all vacation? No chores. No cell phones. No to-do lists. No partially finished house projects staring at me. Get my mind off, and away from, all of life's urgency and demands. Getting rid of the weight of chaos and craziness is emotionally orgasmic and intoxicating.

You know what I mean, don't you? You can feel it too.

You also feel the other shoe is about to drop. Vacations can be imperfect. It rained the week you went to Disney. Or your plane had mechanical trouble, and you missed a connection and didn't make the departure on the cruise. You get the flu the day before you leave. Your kids get sick, and you have to spend the day with them.

Face it! The reality is that most vacations fall far short of perfect. But there's an even bigger elephant in the room. Doesn't it seem a little too Candy-Land to think that the perfect vacation plan for peace will actually make your life peaceful?

You can't get to peace by getting away from reality.

Let's do some math. Assume you get two weeks of vacation every year, and you lump them together in a way that they're perfect and peaceful. It's still only two weeks out of 52. On top of that, the week before vacation is stress-filled because you're expected to finish the work you would have done if you hadn't taken a vacation. So, the first two days of your perfect vacation are spent on recovering and unwinding, so you can't count those. And the last two days of vacation are lost because you're feeling the stress of what's waiting on your desk when you get back and the depressing anticipation of an entire day of sifting through email—which, by the way, assumes you haven't been checking it while you're on vacation in the first place.

So, your two-week escape from reality is actually ten days.

Ten days out of 365—2.7% of your existence. If you work for 65 years in your adult career, that means one and three-quarters of them will be peaceful.

The escape-from-it-all vacation plan is like a child playing peek-a-boo, covering her eyes with her hands to make the adults disappear. You can't get to peace by getting away from reality.

I wonder where we put it. Which drawer is it in? Is it in that box on the top shelf in the back of the closet? Did it get covered up by the pile of laundry and get taken through the wash? Is it under the stack of papers on the desk? Please tell me it didn't get mixed in with the garage sale stuff!

Where could it be?

How could we let something this important get away from us?

He gave it to us, after all. It meant so much to him too. You almost can't talk about him without talking about it. I can see him now in my thoughts, and sure enough, there it is.

His peace. He gave it to us. "Peace I leave with you," he said. "My peace I give you." Would he give it to us if he didn't expect us to keep it? To use it?

To *be* it?

Where in the world did we put it?

And why can't we find it?

I remember that morning and the chill. It was a clear, Texas February morning, a new day.

We'd heard everyone else's stories. What they felt, the complications, the joy, the tension, … *their* stories. But it was our story now.

We were supposed to be at the hospital by 6:00 a.m. There was no traffic. Nothing was moving at that point. Not even him. Brennan was supposed to be born two weeks earlier, but that's not like him. Not that he's always late, he just does things on his own terms, on his own schedule. He's always been that way, even on the day he came into this world.

I'd never been a dad before. I had no idea what to expect. I was excited, but I was more scared than anything else. Scared and helpless.

I was scared for Brennan. There were no indications anything was wrong. Except for being two weeks late, the pregnancy was textbook.

But after being very active early in the pregnancy, he hadn't moved much in the last few weeks. On the other hand, there wasn't much room to move, so … You never know. Until you know. Then you know.

I was scared for Cheryl. She was about to be racked with pain, and there was absolutely nothing I could do to stop it.

In the background, I was scared for myself. Was I ready? Was I up to the challenge? Would I do it right, or would I ruin my kid? What legacy would I leave? How do you do this? I began to long for my dad, who had died many years earlier. I wanted so much to ask him, how … I mean, when things get … I'm not sure how to … what am I supposed to do?

I was glad the highway was nearly empty. Thinking about traffic congestion would have made things worse. Not saying much. Nervous energy. Small talk.

A lot of prayers, though.

Why does it have to happen this way? You're God, can't you do anything? Why does such a joyful time have to be so painful? Why would you curse the process of new life with pain?

Then I remembered—or God reminded me—that once upon a time, in another age, humanity had peace. Peace was all they knew. But then came the terrible day of awareness in the Garden. They wanted more, though they already had it all.

We know chaos because we *are* chaos.

It was their pride that changed peace into chaos. Through pride's eyes, they saw what they could be, though they had no idea it would irreparably change their identity. But it did, and their chaos became ours. We know chaos because we *are* chaos. We are full of …

…pride—striving to make something of ourselves,

…control—jealous to be in charge,

…anxiety—knowing we can't control, though pride tells us we should,

…worry—churning over what bad things might happen because of our lack of control,

…nakedness—concerned about what others will think of us or do to us,

...guilt—knowing we don't measure up, and

...fear—we're afraid of what's outside our ability to manage.

This is who we are. Though we cover it up with a caramel coating of happy thoughts, good intentions and I'm-okay activity, our core remains chaotic.

It is, frankly, convenient to remain chaotic. The normal decisions of life—work, buying houses, building muscles and businesses, determining how many kids we'll have, choosing what we'll eat—don't usually require us to trust much beyond ourselves. Insurance shields us against the bad things in life. Doctors fix us. Drugs take away our pain. Most of the time, the self-reliant mechanisms of life provide just enough of a veneer of peace that we don't have to think about what's in our core.

Then, periodically, we run into a circumstance where self-reliance is inadequate. It's here—in the pain—that we remember. *Don't forget, it's not good to be alone. Don't forget, you had peace once. You were made that way, to be at peace. Remember? It's your original design. It was normal, and it will be normal. It can be normal now if you choose it. If you live it.*

If I become it.

The profoundness of it all hit me full in the chest, and for the next few minutes, I didn't know whether to laugh or cry. As I came back to the awareness that we were driving on the highway, the chill that ran up my spine had nothing to do with the temperature. I'd been shown an anteroom of heaven, a flash of a slice of the side view of eternity. I was between worlds now. It really was a new day, a birth in its own right.

Now 31 years later, I still remember that morning in the car. I feel the chill in the air. I feel the weight of my fear and my false and self-reliant identity suddenly leaving me. The identity that was pushing me to be a man's man and a dad's dad, and the insecurity of trying to be something I can't be apart from God, is gone. Through welling tears, I see relief in the eyes staring back at me in the rearview mirror. I feel my chest expand as I breathe in the first breaths of new life.

Hours later, still trying to absorb the epiphany in the car, I held my new son in my arms and looked at him with devotion and amazement. This new being had his own unique identity, but he belonged to me. I knew he'd always be my son. He'd depend on me to become all God designed him to be.

I realized that chaos would come between us at some point. I wasn't going to be able to make his choices for him or control him. He'd have the freedom to be his own person and potentially choose the wrong path. I'd done that with my dad, and I knew it would be the same for him. The sadness of the thought mixed with the joy of a new son was sobering and forced me to see humanity from God's perspective.

Our rejection of God in the Garden of Eden is akin to us, in a two-year-old temper tantrum, telling God we hate him because we can't get what we want. It's not unlike us being teenagers and dismissing God's fatherly wisdom because we, at a self-determined 18, see him as old school. The stakes were higher, of course, and the consequences more permanent. But the effect was the same—relational chaos.

It seems no accident that God used something so personal and common as the birth of a child to illustrate the break in our relationship with him and the introduction of pain and death into the human condition. He could have used any situation, like:

"You will experience pain when you stub your toe or hit your thumb with a hammer."

"Cancer will test you."

"It will hurt to watch your loved ones deteriorate."

"You will know the chaos of being cheated."

But he chose to associate pain with childbirth. In doing so, he reconciled two seemingly opposite truths into one. On the one hand, the pain of childbirth is a reminder of the consequences of going our own way. On the other, the joy of childbirth reveals the offer of redemption, a chance to see life through the window of restoration and new beginnings. It's the dual revelation that a new life must be *made.* Birthed. And that birth comes at a cost.

It costs me the identity I *think* I want, the one that's so appealing and familiar. It costs me the familiarity of self-reliance, the assumption that I can control life and all its stuff. It costs me the convenience of blaming God when, as the captain of my soul, I'm accountable for steering my life into the storms and the rocks.

That's what's *really* at the core of the peace problem, my self-reliance and self-determination. I have to make peace with the fact that his way is better than mine.

To know peace means a do-over. I have to become a new person, reborn.

I have to exchange my old identity for a new one. I also must face the fact that the exchange rate is high, and I don't make it quickly or easily.

"Follow me," Jesus said to the people who were curious about him. "Whoever wants to be my disciple must deny themselves and take up their cross daily and follow me."

In an age where "follow" means prioritizing someone's social media posts, we have to ask, what does that mean?

Some have over-complicated it, turning it into a legalistic set of rules. Others have over-simplified it, making it cheap, convenient and cliché. In the West, we tend to view religion and faith like we do political parties or maybe sports teams. We're passionate about them. We know the party platforms or our team's style of play. We put stickers on our cars and signs in our yards. We're fans of the key players, and we consume their tweets, posts and media coverage. It's easy to be a fan, the only real cost is buying the T-shirt.

That's what's *really* at the core of the peace problem, my self-reliance and self-determination.

But following Jesus means more than we think it does.

Imagine a large storage bin labeled "My Life." In this bin goes all of life's parts, including your job, marriage, hobbies, chores, exercise, entertainment, etc. If you have a faith tradition or orientation, it's one of the parts in your bin. If you consider yourself to be particularly religious or devoted, your faith part might be the biggest thing in your life bin. You may even have to rearrange the other parts—or perhaps take some out—to get your faith to fit.

If Christianity is your faith tradition, Jesus might be the centerpiece of the faith part. You may take it out of the bin regularly to use it. You've attended church and participated in the programs, sang the songs and prayed the prayers. You know the facts and key Bible verses about Jesus.

This all sounds reasonable, but it's actually—deceptively—wrong.

It's easy to substitute being a fan of Jesus for being a follower of Jesus. Even if faith is the biggest part of our lives, it's still only just a part. And we keep it alongside all the bad stuff of life, the fears, anxieties, greed, disappointment, failures, anger and jealousy. Jesus and his peace can get covered up or even lost.

In asking us to follow him, Jesus is proposing a radical alternative to the "life bin" concept. Instead of Jesus or faith being one of the *parts* in our life bin, Jesus *is the bin* that we put our life into. Following him means making all of our life fit into his identity.

It's easy to substitute being a fan of Jesus for being a follower of Jesus.

He is our life, and all the parts fit and fit together. Everything gets oriented and has purpose, direction, context and meaning.

To metaphorically "take up your cross" (as Jesus himself would literally do) is to willingly engage in bringing your old life identity to an end. A person who's carrying their cross is facing one single and immediate outcome, the surrender of their life. There is no "my life" anymore, that life (figuratively) ends.

"For whoever wants to save their life will lose it," Jesus adds. "But whoever loses their life for me will save it."

It makes sense, after all, doesn't it? How can we live out our new identity when the old one is alive and well?

R.I.P., old identity.

In the days and years since the drive to Brennan's delivery, I've realized how easy it is to wander from the awareness that I must become a new person. I thought the exchange was made that day, the cost was paid and the deal was done.

But it wasn't.

It's like I've become a character in my own *Groundhog Day* movie, where I find myself having to rediscover, through similar experiences, that the exchange was only the first step of a lifelong process. The wholesale change of one day was only the setup for more changes the next day.

"Daily," Jesus qualified. "*Daily* take up your cross and follow me."

Some days, I actually resent it. Like when I go to write this chapter only to realize I'm in a new season of chaos and anxiety. It's so easy to find things to worry about, like getting kids through college, the initial descent and final approach toward retirement, wondering how my body will hold out and whether this book will ever sell and Cheryl's car that's acting up and … so many things.

It's so easy to despair over the chaos in our world. I think of Dexter Filkins' *The Forever War* and his accounts of life in pre-9/11 Afghanistan dominated by the Taliban. As bad as that was, I can only imagine how barbaric it was after they took back the country in 12 days in 2022.

I think of the greed, selfishness and stupidity that triggered the economic meltdown in the financial industry in 2008.

I think of our friend Celia and her Liberian refugee family, who our church helped get settled in America. They'd lived on the run after watching husbands, fathers and brothers be executed by a rival tribe. Now they had to start new lives in affluent America, lost in a strange culture that moved too fast to notice them.

I know of hundreds of thousands of day laborers around the world who couldn't work and faced starvation because of COVID shutdowns—and the ugly prospect that it all could have been the result of experimenting with things we shouldn't have.

I see the pain and distance of a loving, elderly couple whose memories are eroding. Their family is losing them slowly, bit by bit, and day by day.

I ache for the two very close friends who've had children take their own lives.

Despair.

Then there are other days when I appreciate that this faith I follow is a living thing. The chaos in my old identity has deep roots, and the only way to get them out is to be transformed every moment of every day. So, I re-surrender. And on these days, I have Jesus' peace.

Jesus' peace is the fruit of present trust, not past accomplishments. It is not a factoid, an abstract philosophy or random trivia. It's not having positive energy or finding a happy place while playing peekaboo with life's chaos. Peace is not something I purchase or know or possess, it's something *I am*. Peace is a fruit of transformation—it's something I must become.

Peace is a fruit of transformation–it's something I must become.

If.

If we were to get back to that place of peace, that place where new identity is re-birthed daily, then perhaps we'll stop trying to cover up our chaos.

If we approach faith as more than an intellectual exercise, a cultural tradition, a political platform or a set of theological constructs, we can actually change.

Maybe we'll stop pretending to be at peace when we're really not. Maybe we'll stop looking for peace in our circumstances, we'll stop depending on the quick fix, the toys or the get-away vacations that can't remove chaos.

Maybe we'll give up on our self-focus, our lack of compassion and our short temper. Maybe our life won't be so chronic—chronic mouth ulcers, chronic sleep loss, chronic weight gain. We'll get away from the headaches and the depression.

Maybe we'll stop shooting each other in movie theaters and taking advantage of the vulnerable and weak among us. We'll let go of the things that divide us and cause us to despise each other so.

We'll be able to see peace in each other's eyes.

Maybe we'll get back to where we should have been in the first place. That place of trust and security, where our identity is so wrapped in God that even the most trying and tragic of circumstances can't take away our peace.

Maybe, when we make peace with it all, we can offer peace to each other.

Maybe.

DISAMBIGUATION
CHAPTER 6

THE BIG IDEA:

Searching for peace externally to be at peace internally is hopelessly Outside-In. Peace only comes from a new identity—which first requires surrendering the old one.

THE WORLD IS NOT A PEACEFUL PLACE.

It's not just that there's a lot of violence, there's a lack of peace. From couples to countries, we're jealous and resentful. We retaliate and hold grudges, mistrust and protect ourselves. Laws and codes are good, but they don't remove the chaos. Sometimes it's sad, other times, it's tragic.[37]

PEACE IS NOT A PART OF OUR CURRENT IDENTITY.

The lack of peace includes the chaos within us. We know this internal chaos isn't the way it's supposed to be, it's not what we were created to be.[38]

WE TRY TO GET PEACE BY ESCAPING THE CHAOS.

Ignoring or trying to get away from chaos may give us a reprieve, but it doesn't solve the problem. If anything, escaping the chaos only reinforces its reality.[39]

JESUS OFFERS US HIS PEACE.

Of course, if you don't think very highly of him, the offer has little value. If you *do* think highly of him but *don't* have his peace, then something's out of place. Either way, you're missing an opportunity to have peace. And consider this, It's not just any peace he offers. It's *his* peace.[40]

PAIN AND CHAOS ARE REMINDERS THAT WE NEED GOD.

Even in our original state–when all we knew was peace–we still needed God. If we needed him then, how much more do we need him now?

By the way, if "need" seems shameful or weak, consider that you may have either too low a perspective of God or too high a perspective of yourself–or perhaps both. Can we not benefit from the infinite creator of the universe?[41]

GETTING BACK TO PEACE COMES WITH A COST, OUR CURRENT IDENTITY.

The implication of needing God is that we must start over–a rebirth in its own right. The new start requires abandoning our old, broken identity (which is driven by self-reliance and self-determination) in exchange for a new one.[42]

JESUS CALLS US TO COMPLETE SURRENDER.

Jesus offers his peace by following him–reorienting our entire identity around him. Following him doesn't make him a part of our life. It makes him our life. This decision demands some serious reflection.[43]

SURRENDERING IS A DAILY COMMITMENT.

The peace that comes from following Jesus and surrendering our identity is the fruit of present trust, not past or future achievements.[44]

WE CAN ONLY TRULY *MAKE* PEACE WHEN WE'RE *AT* PEACE.

Peace in our world–what we all desire–comes only through individual people becoming peace, then transforming their families, friends, community, region and nation. If we're not becoming peace, the transformation of our world stops–because we can't give away what we don't have. Peace happens when people become peaceful.[45]

PART 3

Altering Life's Rhythms

Saying you want a new identity is one thing. Practicing a new identity in real life is an entirely different thing. The old identity has a lot of baggage.

Chapter Seven

Salt and Light

How does being who you want to be impact those around you?

"WOULD ANYONE LIKE to see the natural color of this cave?" the Mammoth Cave National Park guide asked.

"Yes," I heard my mom reply. I knew something was coming, but my 10-year-old brain wasn't ready for the shock.

I heard a loud metallic clunk and everything disappeared. I saw absolute nothingness. No fade to gray, no shadowy forms of what I had seen just a moment ago. In an instant, I'd lost one of my five senses. Now down to four, I was suffocated by a blackness so thick and immediate I couldn't even sense my mom or dad or my two sisters standing inches from me. The cave, already cold and damp, now added darkness to its qualities and swallowed me whole. For eternal seconds nothing existed, not even me.

Then came another metallic clunk. Instantly the light splashed on the walls of the cave, the blackness fled and reality got its dimensions back. I could breathe. And I knew again that I was—alive.

Now *that* was cool!

Where there is no light, there is only darkness.

Where light is present, darkness ceases.

I've only been to Vegas once. More accurately, I've been *through* Vegas once. Cheryl and I were newlyweds on a one-year offsite assignment in Southern California for my engineering job. We were on our way to Estes Park, Colorado, to meet up with her family for a hiking vacation in one of our favorite spots in the world.

We had decided to travel at night to avoid traffic and the desert summer heat. She was sleeping, and I'd been driving since we left our apartment. Vegas was at the end of our first tank of gas. At the very end.

A city of light in a desert of darkness can't be hidden.

This was back in the day, before Google Maps and turn-by-turn navigation on cell phones. It was getting a little scary driving through the desert after midnight, with our gas gauge hovering at E. I started going over the mileage calculations in my head, pushing aside the sleep that was curling up beside me. I tried to figure out how long it'd been since I saw the last sign, hoping I hadn't run the numbers wrong.

I wondered what it would be like to run out of gas—not a pleasant thought. Life can be unnerving when there's nothing but blackness all around, and you're traveling a lonely highway through an empty desert in a land you've never seen before.

We came over a rise, and there it was—Vegas after dark. Seeing the glow of the city was such a stark contrast to the dimensionless blackness I'd been motoring through for the last several hours. It gave me a bearing. It gave me a destination and hope. One of Jesus' comments came immediately to my mind, "A city on a hill cannot be hidden." In this case, it was a city in a valley, but the illustration was just as vivid. A city of light in a desert of darkness can't be hidden.

From a driving standpoint, Vegas saved us. In a way that road signs, maps and mileage calculations couldn't, the city aglow told us where to go and how to get there.

Come to think of it, I've actually been through Vegas twice. We went through on our return trip—this time during the afternoon rush with plenty of gas. It made for an interesting contrast, a tale of two cities. The first city offered relief and hope, a life-saving place.

This other city offered busyness and traffic hazards. It was a place we had to deal with and get through along the way to our destination. It offered us no real interest.

In fact, it offered nothing.

Light.

There's so much we don't know about it. Scientists still don't know if light is energy or particle-based, it has the qualities of both. Still, light is so practical, so functional. We use light. We've figured out how to turn it on and turn it off. We can focus it into a laser beam, or we can influence our emotions by changing the tone of a room. We heat frozen food and cook popcorn in a box that emits concentrated light beyond our visible spectrum. We peer into space to see the light and measure the universe.

Something tells me we should be careful, though, since this tech knowledge can easily give us a false sense of … something. Command, maybe? Just because we can manufacture light doesn't mean we can create it. We can cheapen it. We can lose the mystery, the beauty that is light.

I've seen some cool lighting effects, but none that can top a good sunset. When the sun sets on a west-facing beach, people stop whatever they're doing to watch. Whether they're eating at outdoor cafes, walking on the beach, or playing volleyball—when the last visible part of the orange ball drops below the horizon, they applaud spontaneously. Even the locals here in St. Pete, who see sunsets on a regular basis, still stop and gaze. And time and again, they even applaud.

I've seen some cool lighting effects on buildings and in rooms, but people don't usually spontaneously applaud for them.

That God spent most of the first day creating light has to make it special. Think of how integral it is to a healthy life, like how light deprivation in winter contributes to Seasonal Affective Disorder (SAD). Think of the way light controls our bodily rhythms by triggering the release of melatonin when it's not around so we can fall asleep and serotonin when it is so we can wake up.

I think it's good that we can use light to suit our own purposes. I think we need to keep our humility about it, though. After all, aren't we better off letting light do its natural work rather than thinking it's all about us?

I don't want to lose the mystery that surrounds light.

I don't ever want to lose the mystery.

A few years back, I attended a business conference with a client. The conference was about how to develop values-based leadership and organizations. The audience was mostly physicians and medical practice managers. One manager of a large practice asked about how to handle a certain physician. This doctor frequently referred to his Christian beliefs, lobbying hard to make faith a central issue in his role and the overall operation of the practice.

There was only one problem.

"He talks all the time about being a Christian. But the way he treats other people makes me wonder what he really believes. He's critical and judgmental. People don't want to be around him. He has a strong belief in his values, but no one else wants those values in the practice because of his behavior. How can I get him to understand that?"

Ouch.

It reminds me of Margaret Thatcher's quote on leadership, "Being a leader is like being a lady. If you have to tell people you are one, you probably aren't." It's a favorite quote because it's so true.

I've worked with people who regularly reminded their direct staff who the leader was. I always thought this was stupid because they were already the leader. Did they think everyone forgot? To be fair, good leadership isn't easy. If it were, there'd be a lot more good leaders around. But when someone has to remind everyone else that they're the leader, it sounds more like they're trying to convince themself.

I've worked with others whose leadership was never in question. They just led, and everyone else just followed. They had the greatest influence, though they weren't the smartest, the loudest, or the most stubborn.

Sometimes they even had a title to go with it, but not always.

I think you could take out "leader" from Maggie's quote and replace it with "Christian," and the idea still works. There's something wrong with having to tell people that you're a Christian. It's like writing "a Christian" on a nametag in the white space right under "Hello, I am," then expecting everyone to be impressed.

When someone has to remind everyone else that they're the leader, it sounds more like they're trying to convince themself.

But it just doesn't work that way. The people I've met that most remind me of Jesus just live, they *are* Christian. In a manner of speaking, you could say they *are* Christ. Maybe not the walking on water part, but they live like him. They don't have to *act* like him, they *are* like him.

Jesus said his followers were salt and light—an interesting pair of metaphors.

Light, as we've already seen, helps people find their way in a dark place. It exposes and reveals, removing doubt, fear and confusion. Darkness ceases to exist when light is around.

In Jesus' day, salt was considered a household staple, along with wine and oil. Since there was no refrigeration, it was used to keep food from spoiling. A pact of friendship was sealed by exchanging salt as a gift. It had medicinal value, and newborn babies were bathed and rubbed in salt.

Salt and light. Environment changers. Preservers of life. Sources of light in darkness. Lovers of enemies. The impact can easily be lost on us who flip a switch to generate light and freeze our food until we're ready to eat it.

Salt isn't like anything else. It's not another compound, like, say, sand, trying to be salty. Though it can be ruined if it gets wet, salt will always be salt.

Light isn't like anything else. It isn't another energy form trying to get to the next level. Though it can be diffused or covered up, light will always be light.

Salt and light influence their world by being what they are. They don't require anything else. They don't *act* like salt and light, they *are* salt and light.

I must admit that I've spent much of my faith journey trying to act like Jesus. I've joined religious systems that spurred me to greater Jesusness. I've worked hard in these systems—harder than many, not as hard as some—to act more like him, in the hope I would eventually be more like him.

It didn't work. It was trying to turn sand into salt. And it probably worked as well as the doctor who went out of his way to tell everyone he was a Christian rather than simply being a Christian.

I was just wearing a nametag.

When I first moved to Canada as a U.S. citizen, I knew I'd experience some cultural differences, but it was hard to pin them down. In my first year there, as I mentioned in Chapter 2, I frequently asked people what it meant to be a Canadian. My friends north of the 49th Parallel found this difficult to answer. Inevitably, they found it easier to describe things about Americans that were un-Canadian.

The greatest clarity came one time when I was in a group that didn't realize I was an American, and the subject of Americans happened to come up.

"Loudmouths," one guy called them, … uh, called *us*.

Another man piped in, "Yeah, they act like they own the place."

"Well," said a third, "That's because they know what's best for everyone else," which elicited a hearty laugh from the group.

Though they were unsure about what a Canadian identity was, they were quick to identify what it was not, American. This seemed backward to me because Canadians have so many great qualities in their national ethos. Canadians are generous, likable people. They're diverse, inclusive and hospitable (except on the hockey rink).

If I were Canadian, I'd define myself by qualities like these.

But then, that's easy for me to say, being an American.

Being on an identity journey prompted me to observe Christians. It was sort of like watching people in the mall or the airport. I had to step out of myself a bit, back away from long-held presumptions and preconceptions, open my eyes … and watch. I saw how people talked about their practices and their interests, their struggles and their joys. I listened to what they did and how they acted.

It was—it is—a little weird.

I see people who call themselves Christians approaching their identity like my Canadian friends by defining themselves by what they aren't. Just listen.

"It's time for Evangelicals to take a more aggressive stance in the political arena."

"The church needs to fight back against the cancel culture."

"*The Shack* is not a Christian book." (This book's dated, but you get my point—every couple of years, some new book creates controversy for Christians).

"Christians should boycott that store because they sell XYZ products!"

"It's not right that Hollywood pushes the LGBTQ agenda?"

"Requiring me to wear a mask violates my freedom of religion."

As you listen, ask yourself why politics and boycotts and issues and controversies are so intoxicating. Why is it so energizing to join in a cause? Is it a coincidence that joining causes is easier than loving others unconditionally—like, say, our enemies? Can we not see that holding *others* accountable is so much easier than holding *ourselves* accountable?

The amount of energy spent highlighting what Christians don't want to be makes me wonder if their primary goal in life is to avoid being un-Christian. It's like advancing Christian interests by attacking things that aren't Christian.

Does salt become salt by trying not to be unsalty?

Would light become more like light by striving not to be dark?

What if we spent our time and energy focusing on what we are—or perhaps better said, what we will be? Wouldn't it be easy to see who we are not? From whatever desert they're traveling through, no matter how dark or dry or hopeless their circumstances are, people could see that our lives are different. They'd ask us where we get our hope, peace and assurance.

Does salt become salt by trying not to be unsalty?

Would light become more like light by striving not to be dark?

Think of the impact that would result if everyone who claims to follow Christ lived this way. What a statement it would make if "Christian" was universally understood to mean "someone who transforms their world through unconditional love." How convincing and influential it would be for Jesus' followers to have one single agenda. Being salt and light—and for this to be the rule, not the exception.

I think it would be cool if people could see *that* identity in Christians. I think living from *that* identity would validate any social or political message we might have. I think more people would see it—especially those who were looking.

We think of love as if it were something we turn on, like a light switch. We think of it as an activity, or maybe a skill or even an emotional expression. When we think of loving others more, we try to work harder at it, looking for a brighter bulb. We think of something we do or should do.

But that's not how I see love in Cheryl.

When it comes to her spiritual awakening, Cheryl's story is pretty vanilla. There's no great turnaround, nothing that God rescued her from. She's never been drunk or high (although it's pretty memorable watching her come out of anesthesia post-surgery). God has never spoken to her from a burning bush. As best she can remember, she's just always followed God.

I've never once felt unloved by her. And I've never seen anyone spend time with her and walk away feeling unappreciated. This isn't something she chooses to do. She doesn't put on love like a shirt or a face of makeup. She doesn't increase the dosage of her love supplement.

She just *is* love.

She'll hate reading this, of course, which is just like her. She'll say she's put her foot in her mouth before. She's offended some people and disappointed others. But those who know her know those are exceptions. And even if they weren't, quantifying them misses the point. Loving others isn't about having the fewest goof-ups or offenses. She's not perfect. But spend time with her, and you'll have the uncanny sense you've been loved—however imperfectly—and you are richer for it.

It's not what you see on the outside that makes her who she is. It's who she is that makes what you see on the outside. Love is an integral part of her identity.

Maybe the best way to measure her love is to watch the effect she has on other people. You can debate the number of her loving characteristics or the quality of her actions, you can't debate the way she makes you feel.

The way she lights up your cave.

I think back to when we met on our blind date. Cheryl, in her boots, led me around the dance floor. That day I rejected what I saw on the outside. She was nice, but frankly, I wanted to leave. My eyes were opened, though, a week later. The dancing blind date was actually a precursor to a weekend double date to attend an Arkansas-Texas A&M football game. We spent three hours trapped in conversation on the drive from Dallas to College Station. She wasn't looking for anything from me. I was important. I was heard. I was relevant. I was respected and valued. All this from a woman who had no romantic interest in me at the time. I began to see who she was on the inside, and it was so captivating I couldn't take my eyes off her. By the end of the weekend, I knew she was the woman I wanted to marry.

I'm reminded of a line from the movie *Gladiator* and Maximus' thoughts on Rome. "Rome is the light," he says. "I've seen much of the rest of the world. It is brutal, and cruel, and dark." For me, love is like Maximus' Rome: Love is the light. Darkness may be the natural color of our cave, but when love appears, the darkness of this world flees. Evil, hatred, pride, fear, hopelessness, trouble, envy, greed, suspicion ... none can remain. In the face of light, darkness has no identity. It has no relevance, no reality.

In the presence of light, darkness ceases.

When I was in seminary, my school hosted a conference and "asked" the students to help out. When I went (late) to sign up, there were only two open slots—one for childcare (a one-hour commitment) and one for serving dinner (two hours minimum). At the time, we'd just had Brennan, so watching someone else's kids was not high on my list of things to do. But childcare would give me one more hour to study—and to sleep. So, I ventured into the fray. Heck, how bad could it be?

In the face of light, darkness has no identity. It has no relevance, no reality.

In the presence of light, darkness ceases.

I'm goin' in—lock and load, baby.

When I arrived at the childcare room, there was a toddler who'd tripped and, unfortunately, broken his fall with his upper lip. It now stuck out like a purple grape. It hurt *me* just to look at it, so I can't imagine how much it hurt *him*. He was absolutely inconsolable. All the other volunteers (who happened to be female) had tried to calm him down, but he had gone off the emotional edge.

I'd never seen him before, but he must have sensed something in me that took away the stranger danger. I looked him in the eye, gave him his blanket, held him close and started talking to him, man to man-cub. Immediately, he quit crying and laid his head on my shoulder. Every minute or so, he would jerk in a deep breath, a leftover reflex from his crying rage.

After five minutes, he suddenly pulled away from my chest, sat up and looked at me straight through, getting a good read.

"Are you for real?" his eyes asked. "Can I trust you?"

We held eyes for a moment, long enough to reassure his young instincts before he laid his head back down. I held him that way for the rest of the hour.

There was a connection between us, and though this may sound like I'm reaching, a manly connection. It wasn't my pity that he felt. It wasn't a consolation technique or a certified childcare skill he recognized. It was something else. I was there, present. I just knew he needed what I had to give. I understood his loss of hope and need for respect amid his pain. I didn't know how I knew it, I just knew. And so did he.

When his mom came to pick him up, he was relieved but didn't immediately clamor for her. And I didn't want to let him go. After a long moment, he knew it was time and simply leaned toward her, replacing my shoulder with hers. Though my hour wasn't up, I left immediately with an eerie confidence that God had steered me to this encounter, and that my job there was done. I felt as gratified as I could ever remember for having helped another human being.

It left a profound impact on me and opened a new understanding of Jesus' priority of love. "This is how everyone will recognize that you are my disciples," he said, "When they see the love you have for each other." It seems that even a child—or maybe *particularly* a child—knows love when he sees it. It's that love radar we all have, the one that works on an intuitive level we can neither justify nor deny.

Love is inexplicable and unreasonable. And unmistakable. It cuts through the crap of this world the way a laser cuts through steel. Nothing can resist it.

And it's something so genuine that we can't just turn it on, you know? It can't be faked or manufactured. There's no such thing as imitation love, synthetic light or artificial salt. Love that's this deep is the visible expression of who we are.

Curiously, though we can't turn it on, we *can* turn it off.

We can't deny it, but we *can* hide it.

Resist it.

Withhold it.

How would we be perceived if love were our most definable, common characteristic?

I wonder.

David Kinnaman's book *unChristian* is a research-based reveal of how people view those who say they are "Christian." The findings are not complimentary. 84 percent of young non-Christians say they know a Christian personally, yet only 15 percent say their lifestyles are noticeably different in a good way. Kinnaman sums up by saying that the negative reaction isn't about what Christians believe, it's about how they behave, the "swagger" and the sense of self-importance they project.

Kinnaman's research summarizes the three most common perceptions of present-day Christianity—anti-homosexual, judgmental and hypocritical. These "big three" are followed by being old-fashioned, too involved in politics, out of touch with reality, insensitive to others, boring, not accepting of other faiths, and confusing.

And this was (as I write this) a decade ago.

Like many, I watched the reports of the Capitol riots at the end of the Trump administration with a spectrum of feelings, from disbelief on one end to disgust on the other. Even more surreal was the involvement of some who claimed their actions were faith motivated.[46] And after the riots, I continued to hear rumblings of protest from some segments of those who identify as Christians that the time has come for more aggressive action against government oppression and restriction of religious freedoms.

How do swagger, mob tactics, self-importance and civil unrest reflect the character, pattern and purpose of Jesus' life? Is Jesus' love somehow insufficient so that we're compelled to enforce it by leveraging social influence and seizing the political high ground?

If so, how do we reconcile this with the fact that Christianity is currently growing fastest in regions where you can be imprisoned or executed for practicing faith in Jesus? And how does that follow Jesus' example of rejecting political influence and power in favor of the much more significant act of loving society's rebels and cast-offs?

Faith or religious beliefs can—and I think should—be a part of the social discourse and political conversation. But this calls for using wisdom and avoiding attempts to protect self-interest or control power. Jesus is calling us to be peace-giving beggars, mourners and meekers, not just for *our* benefit but for the benefit of others. If that's true, we do ourselves a disservice to look at the topic of identity myopically, with ourselves as the sole beneficiary.

Faith, while wholly and personally ours, isn't about us. It's about the object of our faith.

Jesus told his followers that they were light. Not that they'd be *like* light, but that they *were* light. Light, along with salt, doesn't need additional motivation to be what it is. It doesn't need to adapt or develop in order to chase away the darkness. It doesn't need a catalyst or an intervention. It doesn't need a reminder. It doesn't need a majority. It doesn't need government sponsorship—or, for that matter, legal freedom.

Jesus told his followers that they were light. Not that they'd be *like* light, but that they *were* light.

All it needs is a dark place to shine in.

Now *that's* cool!

DISAMBIGUATION
CHAPTER 7

THE BIG IDEA:

Love is who we were meant to be–and there are no shortcuts or artificial substitutes.

DARKNESS CEASES TO EXIST IN THE PRESENCE OF LIGHT.

Light is an element of creation, electromagnetic radiation in the spectrum the human eye can detect. Darkness is … nothing, it's the absence of light.[47]

A "CITY OF LIGHT" CAN'T BE HIDDEN.

If it's truly light, it shines bright. The darker the night, the brighter it shines. It calls to people mired in darkness, who, without light, stumble, trip and fall because they're lost.[48]

TRUE LIGHT IS UNIQUE AND MYSTERIOUS AND SHOULDN'T BE TAMPERED WITH.

If God and Jesus are truly "light"–and his followers, by extension, are ambassadors of light–they must be careful to represent the light in its true form. They would do well to retain the sense of awe and mystery and not look for shortcuts or settle for substitute, sub-standard versions of light.[49]

WE CAN'T BE EFFECTIVE SALT/LIGHT AMBASSADORS BY RE-LABELING WHO WE ARE NOW.

If you tell people you're following Jesus and it's not apparent in your life, something's probably off. Being salt and light is not about wearing a nametag.[50]

WE CAN'T BE AMBASSADORS OF SALT/LIGHT BY BEING LESS OF WHOM WE DON'T WANT TO BE.

Light's brightness doesn't come from trying to be less dark. Trying to represent God by being less of what he's not doesn't make any sense. If we want to represent God and all that he is, we must be like him.[51]

LOVE ON THE INSIDE MAKES US SALT AND LIGHT ON THE OUTSIDE.

Unconditional love is the visible evidence of God living in us. It's the fruit, the natural byproduct of someone who has surrendered their life to him and is living out his teachings. Our love for others points to God.[52]

HOW WOULD CHRISTIANITY BE PERCEIVED IF LOVE WERE ITS MOST VISIBLE, DEFINABLE CHARACTERISTIC?

God only knows. We should consider why Jesus' New Commandment was to love one another as he has loved us.[53]

Chapter Eight

Practically Perfect

How do you make a mystery ... methodical?

I GAVE CHERYL a kiss as I slipped into bed. It was the real deal, slow and deep. You know how words simply fail in tender moments? This was such a moment. After I pulled back from her lips, still face-to-face, I let out a sigh and let my eyes speak.

"Your beauty shines like a thousand full moons," they proclaimed.

"Your hair falls on your shoulders like layers of satin."

"Your smile thrills me, melts me and sends my heart spinning."

"You are the joy of my life, and I love you so much."

The ladies dig those loving gazes, you know. I expected her eyes to say something back to me, but it was her mouth that spoke.

[Insert the sound of a needle scraping across a record]

"Did you brush your teeth?"

It really sucks that you can't smell your own bad breath. How can you miss the concoction of vinegar, stale coffee and sweaty socks that emanates from the mouth right under your own nose?

I posed that question to a doctor one time. He told me that we get so familiar with the smell of our own breath that the stinky part simply doesn't register. We end up with an olfactory blind spot, where the smell is so usual, we believe it to be normal.

We end up with an olfactory blind spot, where the smell is so usual, we believe it to be normal.

That means most of the time you're probably walking around with everyday, run-of-the-mill bad breath you can't detect.

But don't worry. Other people can smell it, even if you can't.

Where did I put those breath mints?

I've always had trouble with the difference between "its" and "it's." I don't know why. All my "it's" get apostrophes, whether they need them or not. My friend Shannon, who used to proofread for me, finally got tired of circling all my "it's" with her red pen.

"You've got a lot of "it's" in there," she vented.

"Yeah, I know. I have trouble seeing those."

"I-t-*apostrophe*-s is the contraction of 'it is,'" she continued.

"Yeah, I know."

"Well, obviously not."

"No, you don't understand. I know the rules, but I guess I have the habit of adding an apostrophe every time."

"Then stop it."

"I know! That's what I tell myself. But when I proofread my writing, I don't ever see them, it's like I'm blind to them."

"Well, just remember that when you're…" Once again, she began to refresh the rules on apostrophe usage. She didn't quite know what else to say because there wasn't much else she could say.

When I hand off something to be proofread, it always comes back marked up. Always. It's not like I'm suicidal over it, but I'm amazed that something I'm so focused on can be filled with glaring mistakes. My last book, *In the Way*, required six rounds of proof-editing—the last one, after finding typos in the "final" proof, had been approved and submitted for production! There's no escaping the imperfections. It's called *proof.* The red marks glare at me like an eyewitness pointing out the perpetrator, "That's the man! He's the one who did it!"

I must admit that this frustrates me. Don't get me wrong—I want my writing to be the best it can be, so I'll do whatever it takes to make it better. But writing is about the content, right? Can't you pick up my intent, my heart? The *message* is what's really important here, not some extra apostrophe. Can't a writer get a break?

Every now and then, I catch a typo in a published book.

"Can you believe this?" I'll say to Cheryl if she's within earshot. "This typo made it through all those layers of edits. I can't understand why no one caught this, it's so obvious."

I guess I'm not the only imperfect writer, after all, huh?

I can't decide if what I feel is indignation or justification.

I think it says something about human nature that there are so many different religions and groups within those religions and subgroups within those groups. Even Christianity—with Jesus as the definitive, unified standard—has a variety of distinct flavors.

It seems to me that this divisive tendency is a spiritual blind spot. After all, if there is one God, wouldn't it make sense that all who seek him would acknowledge and operate by his standard? We agree on other standards, like an inch is an inch to everybody, even to people who prefer centimeters. Why is it so hard to imagine one acceptable standard for following God? One standard we all hold to without segueing into cliques and clubs.

But instead, we take the standard and break it down into parts. We adjust, shift, highlight and reprioritize. Then we create a preferred language, define the (un)acceptable activities, attach a few behavioral metrics, stir vigorously and voila! We have our new standard.

Our approach.

Of course, we forget that our standard is only *part* of the true Standard. At best, it's *sub*-Standard, a facsimile. But since it's fairly close to the original, it works—for *us*. It works *for* us and *against* any who don't adhere to our sub-Standard.

Because it works, it satisfies our urge to rate ourselves. Our approach, our standard, is *almost* perfect. It's *not* perfect, of course. But it's as perfect as it can be—for us.

And it's practical, functional, easy maintenance, definable and turnkey.

Practically perfect.

There are several disturbing things about this practical perfection. One is that our practically perfect approach hides the opportunity to be transformed. After all, if we can get by on *practical* perfection, why do we need *genuine* perfection?

You get so familiar with your practical perfection that these holes simply don't register.

Another is our propensity to compare standards. We like it when our sub-Standard is better than someone else's sub-Standard. It makes you wonder whether we create our standards not to position ourselves relative to God but to position ourselves relative to each other.

Hmmm, let's park that thought and come back to it later.

The final disturbing thing is that there are holes in our practically perfect approach. There are compromises and contradictions that don't quite add up and issues that we haven't fully resolved. Ironically, it's usually easy for others to see the holes in our approach that we can't.

It's almost like you get so familiar with your practical perfection that these holes simply don't register. It's like having a spiritual blind spot, where the inconsistencies are so usual that you believe them to be normal.

That means most of the time you're probably walking around with an everyday, run-of-the-mill, practical perfection you can't detect.

But don't worry. Other people can see it, even if you can't.

There's a story in the Bible about when God was giving his standard to the Israelites. Moses had gone up the mountain to talk to God. He'd been gone a long time, and the Israelites became impatient. They wanted some action, so they went to Aaron to get things going.

"C'mon," they said, "Do something!"

"Like what?" Aaron reacted.

"Like we should know? You're Moses' right-hand man. Can't you come up with something?"

Aaron considers, then evades, "How about we just wait a little longer?"

"How about *not?*" someone volleys. "No one knows what happened to Moses. For all we know, he died in that fire on the mountain. Who are we going to follow now? All those miracles—the dividing-the-sea thing, the water out of a rock—those were weeks ago. There's no guarantee we'll get any more miracles without him. We can't wait around here forever, doing nothing. We need to get on with the program! You need to make up something we can follow."

"What do you want me to do, *make up* a god?"

"Hey, now there's an idea."

"Yeah, a *stupid* idea. How are we going to make up a god to replace God?"

"No, not to *replace* God—to *symbolize* him, to *elevate* him. Think about it: We know God exists. We know what he's like, and we should honor that. But we need to do our part—we need to show him off, so people will be impressed and want to know more about him."

"And besides, 'God helps those who help themselves,' right? I know God never actually said that, but work with me on this: He wants us to go to the Promised Land. Well, we can't do that sitting here, can we? We know what he wants us to do, so let's do it!"

"Okay," Aaron softens. "I see what you mean. Let's put our heads together and make something that represents God. That'll encourage everyone! It'll help them remember that God is still here. It'll remind us of who God is and what we're supposed to do."

"Yeah, baby!" they exclaim. "Now we're cooking with gas!"

Aaron picks up the pace. "Great! So, let's start with all your jewelry. We'll melt it down and come up with an image. Hmmm, what image though … I know! We'll use a bull! Everyone knows that powerful gods ride bulls. We'll make the biggest, baddest, meanest bull anyone's ever seen. It'll be better than all those wimpy bulls that represent the gods everyone else worships."

"Very cool!" the crowd said. "We'll have the best bull ever. Nobody's bull is better than our bull!"

So, they made the bull. Then they built an altar, a place of worship where they could come together and talk bull. They ate and drank on the bull's behalf. They partied and fellowshipped because of the bull. It was all about the bull.

Then the bull party got a little out of hand and started looking less like church and more like ... well, things that don't represent God at all.

And God thought it was all a bunch of bull crap.

How do you represent perfection?

Jesus took an interesting approach. "Unless your righteousness surpasses that of the Pharisees," he claimed, "you will not enter the kingdom of God." Why would Jesus use his arch-enemies—the ones who would eventually plot and pull off his execution—as a point of reference for something he was trying to promote?

In Jesus' day, the Pharisees were the prime example of living out a practically perfect approach to life and spirituality. Their devotion to God was commendable.

And extreme.

They formed after the Israelites returned to Judea after the Babylonian exile, intending to rebuild the lost heritage of God's chosen people. These "separated ones" promoted exclusivity and a worldview where every aspect of life fell under the rule of God—to which they became the gatekeepers.

"We'll have the best bull ever. Nobody's bull is better than our bull!"

They were in a prime position to lead a movement of restoration back to Yahweh, but over time their solemn devotion to righteousness and social reformation turned into a sick, elitist, empowered clique. They ended up with the tightest, cleanest religious ethic you could ever put together. They wanted to prepare Israel to receive the Messiah they believed was soon coming. And they worked at it so diligently that when he actually showed up, they killed him.

What is perfect like? I can think of a few things.

My daughter's smile, for starters. I mentioned this once before (and I admit some bias here, being a dad), but it's perfect. Not the one she puts on when the camera comes out. I mean the *perfect* one—the one that blooms when she's really happy. It starts like a rosebud in the corner of her mouth, then blossoms in an instant, all full of the fragrance and color of joy. Her smile is perfect until you ask her to smile for the camera, then it's not.

My son's humor, for another. Ryan has the gift of comedic timing. He just says things in a way that cracks people up. Sometimes I try to copy him, but it never really works for me. I've asked him how he does it, to teach me so I can be funny, too. But he can't explain humor.

"Dissecting the frog, Dad. Remember?" he could admonish, "It usually kills the frog."

My grandmother's lemon cake is another picture of perfection. Her name was Oleta (pronounced as "Oleeta"). Oleta baked a melt-in-your-mouth perfect lemon cake. No one could copy it.

My siblings and I asked her several times for the recipe.

"Oh, you add a little bit of sugar, and some lemons of course. And a few other things. You know, it's just a cake."

Pfft, fat chance. Though the best of our attempts tasted good, they were never Oleta's. Of course, she never gave out the recipe. In fact, there never was one, perfection doesn't come from a recipe.

Sex is perfect, even though often it's not, and sadly it's frequently abused. Sex reminds you that you're dabbling in something bigger and more powerful than you ever thought possible.

Great writing has a quality of perfection about it. Do you know how good authors paint perfect pictures with imperfect words? Great writing is perfect in a way that can't quite be measured.

It took Michelangelo four years to paint the Sistine Chapel. It's claimed that at one point, he was so disillusioned he wanted to give up. He despised his work and lamented his lack of skills as a painter. Hardly a description of perfection.

I've never seen the Sistine Chapel, but friends who have seen it say it is breathtaking beyond description. It redefines the word *masterpiece*. Imperfect though it may be, when we look at it, we see perfection, maybe not the perfection of art, but the art of perfection.

I can say these things are perfect, though they're not.

God is perfect, too, but his perfection is total and complete. This is both comforting and distressing. It's comforting because I prefer to worship a deity worthy of the claim and distressing because this is the standard to which he calls me.

"Be perfect," Jesus says, "as your heavenly father is perfect."

It's intimidating to imagine a God who is the perfection I can't be. He never makes a typo. He never needs a breath mint. He has the luxury of never feeling guilty because he's never screwed up. I want to be perfect that way, I really do. But I can't. And because I can't, God's perfection distresses me. And Jesus' challenge sounds like a setup, a big case of spiritual entrapment.

But my perspective on perfection is different from God's. He doesn't see perfection through measuring typos and bad breath.

I look at perfection as a scorecard. He looks at perfection as a state of being.

I look at perfection as something I've never attained. God looks at perfection as something he's never lost.

I look at perfection as performance. Try harder and suck less. God looks at perfection as identity, made in his image.

I look at perfection as a scorecard. He looks at perfection as a state of being. Complete. Sound. Whole. Stable. Total. Thorough. Firm. Fit. Unimpaired. Robust. Solid. Intact. Right. Safe. Sane. Substantial. Unblemished. Vital. Integral. Flawless. Ideal.

Perfect.

True enough, there *is* an inescapable challenge when Jesus says, "Be perfect, as your heavenly Father is perfect." There's also, when I listen deeply, an invitation.

It's an invitation to a perfection I can live out in this life, though technically, I'm not there yet. It's a perfection that doesn't point to me—as if it were all about me. Instead, it's a perfection that points *through* me, beyond me, to something else, the way Hannah's smile or the Sistine Chapel or sex points to something bigger, deeper. It's a perfection no human approach could ever produce because capital-P Perfection doesn't come from a recipe. It's the perfection I thirst and hunger for as a beggar-mourner-meeker. It's the perfection God desperately wants us to be restored to—and he's provided a way to achieve it.

It is, I think, the great challenge in living by faith. To willingly dismiss the caramel coating of my own practical perfection that seems so right, so real and so true—and (relatively speaking) so comfortable and attainable. It's a challenge to trust that God will give his perfection to me on the condition that I follow him and embrace his resolution to my imperfection problem.

I can't go back.

I can't go back to building a practically perfect, Outside-In approach that won't perfect me. I have no more energy to give to a system that justifies blindness to my own gaps, that rewards my comfort with spiritual breath that smells bad to everyone but me.

I can no longer commit to a practically perfect, Outside-In approach that promises to clear my conscience but instead leaves a patina of guilt that won't wash away. It promises attainable perfection and freedom but instead shackles my conscience in a prison where it can no longer detect my hardened heart toward God, my hollow attitudes toward others and my pride that's covered by a veneer of false humility.

History is full of people who justified themselves and their practically perfect, Outside-In approach, sometimes to despicable extremes, like Medieval Christianity that authorized the Inquisition and the Crusades, Isis, southern "Christian" slave owners, the Nazis, …

And me.

Maybe not to the same extent, but it's the same process, isn't it?

To the degree that my approach shapes my conscience, God's Spirit cannot—and will not. With a practically perfect approach in place, real perfection is a distant fantasy, an irrelevant nuisance. And as long as my conscience remains imprisoned by a practically perfect approach, I will never be transformed.

I will never be who I want to be.

I can't go back to diligently practicing an Outside-In approach that over-prioritizes self. When my world of perfection revolves around the pole of self-interest, it becomes a burdensome chore to respect others, ask for forgiveness or love them as Jesus loves me. My approach has no protocol for humility.

I can't go back to a spirituality of my own making, a manufactured idol that I promote as God-honoring and that seems right in my own eyes—my own practically perfect eyes. After all, a less-than-Perfect approach is really just a bunch of bull crap.

To the degree that my approach shapes my conscience, God's Spirit cannot–and will not.

I won't go back to a recipe that produces predictable results, no matter how tasty and tempting the imitation may be. Perfection is made from scratch, it's customized and created.

I can only go forward toward Perfect and leave behind my practically perfect, Outside-In approach. The path to Perfection is too narrow for such a wide load, anyway.

That God has created a way for us (who aren't perfect) to be perfect is radical beyond belief. It's perfection by proxy, in the person of Jesus Christ. As I continually reject my convenient, practically perfect sub-standards, I have greater clarity to see his Perfection.

After nearly 40 years of stumbling forward in following Jesus in faith, I've realized the closer I get to him, the more I see my imperfection. I'm a self-interested jerk in my innermost, natural self—the part that remains until my full liberation is complete. Though this might sound depressing or even self-mutilating, it's counter-intuitively liberating. It's a truth that my prior orientation to faith never allowed me to see. I'm being transformed, step by step, so that I resemble Jesus instead of my sub-standard imitations of him.

Faith in Jesus allows me to live out the paradox of simultaneously seeking perfection and experiencing perfection. As the Bible says, "For by one sacrifice he has made perfect forever those who are being made holy."[54] Anything in me that's good or wholesome is not me, it's Jesus in me. And I've never felt more comfortable, free, purposeful or relevant in my entire life.

It's like Michelangelo said, "The greater danger for most of us lies not in setting our aim too high and falling short, but in setting our aim too low, and achieving our mark."

Maybe he realized this during the four years he lay on his back working on the art of perfection, or maybe not.

Either way, it seems what's true for art is true for identity as well.

DISAMBIGUATION
CHAPTER 8

THE BIG IDEA:

Our religious approaches can easily corrupt our understanding of God and the identity he has intended for us to experience.

IT'S NATURAL TO BECOME BLIND TO OUR IMPERFECTIONS.

We live with them every day, encountering them so frequently that we simply embrace them as normal.[55]

EVEN IN OUR IMPERFECT STATE, WE'RE CRITICAL OF OTHERS.

We tend to give ourselves the benefit of the doubt and withhold it from others. It's silly, but obvious, we evaluate others according to a relative standard we create–one that, ironically, we ourselves don't often meet.[56]

IT'S HUMAN NATURE TO CREATE A PRACTICALLY PERFECT, OUTSIDE-IN RELIGIOUS APPROACH.

It's both functional (practical) and aligned with our beliefs (perfect)–it's practically perfect. Practicing this Outside-In approach does three things: 1) It hides our own imperfections, 2) it positions us to compare ourselves with each other, and 3) it anesthetizes our need for transformation.[57]

OUR PRACTICALLY PERFECT APPROACH CORRUPTS OUR UNDERSTANDING OF GOD.

Using an Outside-In approach to make ourselves right blinds us from seeing the breadth of God's perfection—and our imperfection. Any part of a practically perfect approach that falls short of God's perfection represents him falsely. It tricks our conscience into believing everything's okay, and it severs our connection to who we really want to be.[58]

GOD CALLS US TO HIS PERFECTION, A RETURN TO OUR ORIGINAL IDENTITY.

Jesus' call to be perfect (as God is perfect) can sound like an over-the-top, unachievable requirement. Many have tried to establish perfectionistic religious ethics, like the Pharisees of Jesus' time and many others since. But Jesus wasn't calling us to *upgrade* our Outside-In approach, he was calling us to *abandon* it. No approach of our making can perfect us. Instead, he offers *his* perfection.[59]

GOD'S PERFECTION CAN ONLY BE RECEIVED WHEN WE TRUST AS A WAY OF LIFE.

Embracing the depth of our imperfection and our incapacity to make ourselves perfect is a necessary step. But it's just one step in what must become a new way of life where we fully trust in God rather than ourselves.[60]

Chapter Nine

I'll Be the Judge of That

Who are you in comparison to other people?

IT WAS TYPICAL Florida July weather. The Gulf of Mexico simmered at 90 °F, the air hyper-saturated. The ground, unable to absorb heat like the ocean, radiated it upward elevating the wet air to the cold reaches of the atmosphere's penthouse.

These conditions create rivers of air flowing upward that would be invisible were it not for the condensation. Once at altitude the rivers widen, boiling and blossoming into giant angry anvils.

I'd long ago gotten used to the late afternoon Florida thunderstorms. As the locals can attest, you need to be wrapping up your outdoor activity around 3:00 p.m. because it's going to start raining somewhere. Maybe not where you are, but one mile away it might be coming down in buckets.

I'd gotten used to the storms, but not the lightning that comes with them. After all, they didn't name the world champion Tampa hockey club just for being fast with the puck. There are only two other places in the world that have higher lightning density than Tampa Bay.

Obviously, it's impossible to know where lightning's going to strike. That's especially true in Florida because it could hit anywhere, since it's so flat. Even the slightest elevation makes you look like a lightning rod. So you certainly don't want to be around anything that conducts electricity.

Like metal.

Or water.

Or metal sticking out of water.

It wasn't storming at our house yet this evening, but it was booming to the south.

That's when I got the call. I was on the pastoral staff at a church, and the call was from a fellow pastor, John Marc. He was the point of contact that week for pastoral emergencies. He said someone had called the church and left a strange voicemail—for me.

"You *really* need to call her back—*now*."

Uh oh.

The message played back the terse, on-duty voice of a Hillsborough County deputy.

"We've got one of your parishioners up here on the Sunshine Skyway Bridge, and he's threatening to jump. We've been talking to him for a couple of hours now. And I don't know how much more we can do to convince him. He said you are his pastor. If there's any way you can get up here to help us, I'd like you to come immediately."

The parishioner's name was Mitchell. He and his wife had recently started attending our church, and I'd only talked to him briefly after the service. They had just had their first child and were coming to church to help figure out this next chapter in their lives.

Then things went all sideways.

The baby was colicky, and one night Mitchell apparently lost his temper. The child ended up comatose with shaken-baby syndrome. The marriage broke up and Mitchell was charged with aggravated child abuse. Facing up to 30 years in prison and a lifetime of guilt for a moment's loss of control, it must have seemed like a reasonable solution to jump off the Skyway.

Which is one of the tallest structures in Tampa Bay.

It's also made of metal, in the middle of a large body of water.

And it just happened to be ground zero for this evening's thunderstorm.

I jumped in the car and began racing down the interstate, trying to figure out how to convince him that what seemed reasonable was anything but. The spits of rain soon became sheets, making it difficult to see. I quickly found myself in the back of a 10-mile traffic jam, a result of stopping the traffic on the bridge at the tail end of rush hour. I pulled onto the shoulder, driving as fast as I dared and hoping there wasn't any debris or abandoned cars that I'd hit before I'd see.

People were honking, some even feigning pullouts to stop me. I could feel their curses. It dawned on me that I was now one of those impatient shoulder drivers I'd felt disdain for in the past.

I finally got to the tollbooth at the base of the bridge and asked the attendant for the latest news, which she obviously had repeated many times already.

"Yeah, we've got another jumper. There's nowhere to go."

Another? Man, how often does this happen?

"Yes ma'am, I know. I'm a minister, and he's one of my parishioners. The Sheriff's office called me, and I've got to get up there."

"Oh, okay. Well, come on through. And good luck."

By the time I got up there, it was too late—in a good sense. The officers had talked Mitchell off the edge. He'd been there over four hours, one leg over the side, 197 feet above the rocks at the base of a main column. Had he jumped, he'd have been nothing more than a statistic.

I'm sure it was a tortuous four hours for him, dealing with the guilt of it all. Feeling the judgment, the shame. Even the people stuck in their cars were yelling for him to jump. No doubt the reality of his choices hit him in the gut, over and over again. Maybe it was an elaborate penance, a desperate way to validate himself. Maybe this was even a twisted, backward way to tell his wife and child how much he loved them—though the child would never understand the gesture.

But I didn't *do that to my child,* did *I?*

How low do you have to think of yourself for that to be a solution?

Maybe if I'd done that to my child and my family, I'd know.

But I didn't *do that to my child,* did *I?*

It was the end of a long day, one in a countless string of long days and short nights. The days get like that with young kids. Reality and time compress, perspective shallows and life gets grey and two-dimensional. You're Numb. Reactive. You function on the sheer power of will to get up and keep going. I could hear my mom's voice in my head, reminding me that "Havin' kids is how you pay for your own raising."

Maybe tonight. This could be the night I get some sleep.

Thinking about sleep is both a blessing and a curse. It's hopeful to look forward to sleep. But the ray of hope is squashed by the reality that sleep so often gets interrupted. It's almost better not to think about it. If sleep comes, it will be a bonus, if not, there's always tomorrow.

I was driving home, probably from the store to get milk. And diapers, always more diapers. It had been raining, which was normal for Vancouver. In the Pacific Northwest, most of the time it was either raining or it had just been raining. It was also a bit on the cool side. Cool enough that the rain and the dark together felt lonely and heavy.

My son Ryan was with me. Probably to get him out of the house, and give him a change of scenery. He was around four years old at the time. It's always been easy to tell Ryan's mood, since he's usually extraverted with his feelings. He was particularly transparent as a toddler. Whatever emotion was ripe at the time got lived out. High highs, and low lows.

This night was a low. He'd been griping and whining about everything. He was convinced that life was bad, and he was letting everyone in on his world.

Finally, I'd had enough.

"If you don't stop griping, you can walk home. Is that what you want?"

We were in our neighborhood, with no traffic, and just around the corner from the house, some natural consequences just might get his attention.

"Yeah," he said with four-year-old defiance. To him, it was a game, some kind of new adventure. He was rubbing it in my face. *I'll show you! You can't make me be happy!*

"Okay, fine. Have it your way."

I jerked the van to a stop, got out and walked around to the side. I slammed the door open, and his eyes told me he suddenly realized this game wasn't going to be much fun. The satisfaction poured over me like a hot shower. Invigorated and justified, I yanked him from his booster seat, plopped him by the curb and slid the door closed with a purpose.

"I'll see you at home." I got back in the car and began to drive away, looking in the mirror where objects are further away than they appear, especially on cool, misty nights.

"Daddy!?!?"

It is a sound forever burned into my consciousness, a mix of confusion and terror. And abandonment.

It is the sound of one of my greatest failures as a parent.

I slammed on the brakes and ran back to him, still standing where I plopped him in the cold, wet shadows. I embraced him as I never had. I'm not sure who needed the embrace more—me or my son, who now clung to me as if I was his hero.

Hero. *Yeah, right.*

The rain had stopped, and the storm had lost interest in the drama and moved on to dampen someone else's evening. I stood by the remaining band of emergency vehicles and troopers filling out reports in their cruisers. I looked out over the waters of the Bay, ominous and inky, swallowing light as easily as they would have swallowed a life.

And wondered.

What must Mitchell be going through? Think about it. You live your life as a normal adult, trying to make it all work. Then, in a moment of fatigue and stupidity, you do the unimaginable. If you could only have it back, you'd be a normal guy again.

But there's no do-over. It's an instant frozen in time that becomes a portrait of your new identity. Forevermore, the bad guy.

I can relate to the illogic, the frustration and the emotional drain that anesthetized his common sense. I hurt for him and the pain he must feel for the family he failed, the wife whose trust he betrayed and for his baby, who will never experience a normal life.

That's one part of me.

But there's another part of me, wily and shrewd.

"What drives a parent to do something so selfish, so cruel? Is the baby crying just to irritate you? You think the baby is enjoying *his colic?"*

He antes up in the conversation, raising the stakes. He's awkwardly ambivalent. He brings a cold satisfaction, an odd sense of justice that distances me comfortably from grace. He fans into flame a karma-esque attitude that Mitchell got his comeuppance, a guilty verdict that feels oddly satisfying.

He brings a cold satisfaction, an odd sense of justice that distances me comfortably from grace.

He keeps buddying up to me, all chummy-like. I don't really like him, and I don't tell my friends about him.

But I never really put him off, either.

It makes for a kind of co-dependent security blanket. I both despise and embrace him—I despise his simplistic cruelty, yet embrace the way he elevates my self-worth and justifies my actions. I frown on his condemnation of others, yet find comfort in his reassurance that I'm right. I regret the speed and severity of his verdicts, yet I find confidence in his clarity.

I don't talk about this part of me. But secretly, I'm in love with him.

What is it about other people's stuff that is so captivating? Why is it so easy to see their faults? How is it that I understand their motives so well?

It must be a gift.

"Why do you look at the speck of dust in your brother's eye?" came a different voice, whose tone was different from my judging companion's voice. The abruptness of it made me uncomfortable.

"Well, … uh … I'm not sure what you mean."

"What do you think I mean?"

"Uh … that I'm focusing on insignificant things?" I offered.

He redirected, "Do you think your brother *enjoys* that speck in his eye?"

"I don't think so. It bugs the crap out of me when the wind blows something in my eye and I can't get it out."

"Yeah, that makes sense, doesn't it? So it *is* significant."

"So what's the problem, then?"

"What do *you* think the problem could be?"

Geez, so many questions.

"Look," I challenged, "I'm not sure where you're going with this. I'm trying to help this guy. If he could just see what I see, he'd do things differently, you know? He'd change. I think his life could be so much different. I've seen this before. I know he's gonna regret it."

"Yeah, you're probably right."

"So do I just stand there and do nothing, while he creates trouble for himself? Pretend like I don't care? That doesn't seem right."

"I agree, it doesn't."

"So what's the answer?"

"Why do you look at the speck of sawdust in your brother's eye, and pay no attention to the log in your own eye?"

"That's a question, I asked for an answer."

"That *is* an answer," he corrected.

Pushback time. "No, that's a question. See how your voice went up at the end? See that little curly symbol after the statement? It's called a 'question *mark*.' It's always used with a question."

"No, it's an answer, it's just not the answer you were looking for."

Then came the pause and what felt like him leaning closer. It wasn't my eyes that saw the look on his face. The suddenness of it all caught my soul naked.

"It's not the answer *you wanted to hear.*"

I think I liked it better when he was asking questions.

"So," Jesus repeated, "How can you say to your brother, 'Let me take the speck out of your eye,' when you can't see past the log in your own eye?"

I didn't answer, but he didn't wait for my answer.

"What do you call someone who claims to have qualities he doesn't actually possess?"

Another pause.

"What do you call people who say one thing and do the opposite? Someone who lives one way on the outside and a different way on the inside? You've been to seminary. What do you call someone who puts on a mask and pretends to be what he's not?"

"A hypocrite," my answer came before I realized the weight of it all. It was like taking the big box labeled Packing Peanuts off the top shelf without realizing it was full of rocks.

"It comes from the Greek word for 'actor,' right?" he reminded. "*Hupokrites*—someone who's acting a part? Playing a role in a make-believe reality? Tell me, making a judgment call on someone else's issue without first dealing with your own issues? Who are you trying to be? Are you trying to be Me?"

I had no answer.

"Are you capable of being what I Am?"

There was no answer.

"You, hypocrite," Jesus gracefully but truthfully summarized, "first take the log out of your own eye, and then you'll see clearly to remove the speck from your brother's eye."

Hypocrite.

The admonition stings and the slap is abrupt and uncompromising. It pulls back the covers on the secret love of my life, on my artificially high perception of self that takes the seat of the righteous Judge.

Its bite is a ready reminder that Jesus' harshest criticism centered on hypocrisy. There are few things that God hates more than hypocrisy—except, maybe, pride or a lack of concern for the poor or helpless.

The admonition stings and the slap is abrupt and uncompromising.

Hypocrisy calls for such a rebuke.

The Pharisees got the brunt of it in the Gospels. In one exchange, Jesus called them whitewashed tombs. They're gleaming white on the outside yet full of defiling, decaying death on the inside.

It'd be interesting to know how the Pharisees talked about their ancestors—the ones who built the golden calf and did all the bull crap.

I wonder if the Pharisees talked about their ancestors as critically as we talk about the Pharisees today.

Huh … I wonder.

There are rats in Florida.

Our house was in Florida.

We had rats in our attic.

We'd tried just about everything to get rid of them, including poison, traps, bait, sealant on the gaps and wire mesh on the openings. They kept finding their way in. We could've burned the house down, but that's a cutting-off-the-nose-to-spite-the-face thing and (because they're rats) they'd have gotten out, anyway.

We have a friend, Robert, who owns a wildlife control business. Robert knows his rats. He helped us get rid of our rats by spraying our attic with this foggy mix that smells like cinnamon and sweaty socks. It's really cool because it's non-toxic and non-poisonous. The active ingredient is a microbe that eats rat urine. It turns out that rats dribble urine as they walk around in your attic, which they use to tell themselves where they've been. Once the urine is gone, they can't navigate anymore. They know something's not right, so they leave. And never come back.

Like rats leaving a sinking ship.

"Rats are the ultimate survivors," Robert explained. "They have a sixth sense about threats, and they'll do anything it takes to survive."

"Really?" I asked. "How so?"

"Well, if huddling together and procreating is what it takes to survive, *that's* what they'll do—and they do *that* very well, by the way," he added with a smirk. "But if they sense there are too many rats for the available food, they'll eat each other to survive. Rats really don't care about anything but survival. They only think about themselves."

Companies have brands. Nike has a brand. Walmart, Bank of America and Apple, they have brands. People have brands. Beyonce has one. Even Hitler had one. We all have a brand, maybe not as famous as Beyonce's or as infamous as Hitler's. But we have one.

A brand is a public perception, what people think of when they hear your name. Brand management, then, is about shaping that perception. It's about giving people something to associate with you, to believe and feel about you.

It's your brand, and it's what you want people to see. But managing your brand has limits because people will see what they want to see—whether you want them to or not. As I thought about Mitchell and his brand, I wanted to condemn him for what I'd seen but couldn't. The alternative—excusing him—didn't seem acceptable. Oddly enough, I didn't feel the drive to do either. I felt paused.

With "Daddy!?!?" reverberating in my head, instead of picking apart his brand, I kept seeing my own. I became aware of a kind of gravity pulling me toward a slippery slope whose fall line goes like this:

- When something or someone is different, it's easy to misunderstand.
- When I misunderstand, it's easy to presume—especially about motives.
- When I presume, I then devalue.
- When I devalue, I resent.
- When I resent, I despise.
- When I despise, I judge.
- When I judge, I position myself as superior and worthy to make the judgment.

I realized I was looking down the slope that bottoms out in a place I didn't want to be, though it felt so much like home. I was elevating my own brand at his expense.

It's a prison, really, like an addiction. It's the boudoir of my secret, co-dependent lover. He brings me what I want, and I hate him for it. It feels so miserably natural, the reward so desirably disgusting.

At the bottom of this slope, at the end of this process, I don't like who I am.

Standing on the Sunshine Skyway Bridge, now well past sunset, I stared into the inky waters of Tampa Bay. A humid, salty sea breeze left my face and hands feeling tacky. I wanted to feel satisfied with my effort to help Mitchell. But the satisfaction was hollow and opportunistic because it required me to equate him with his actions. It wanted to credit me for doing something good for someone … how could you say it … undeserving, perhaps? It called for me to judge Mitchell.

Judging others is really insecurity over my own identity.

I couldn't take that step, though everything in me wanted to. With my secret lover whispering in my ear that I was a good man, the inky waters were a kind of looking glass. They reflected back the image of a man prolonging his own survival by feeding off another's mistakes and misfortune. I saw the slippery slope and gravity of judgment and its lust for increasing market share for my brand. I saw its hyper-focus on the perception of the caramel coating. How others perceive me and how I perceive myself.

I saw that judging others is really insecurity over my own identity.

Jesus called his followers to love and serve, to build up and encourage, to walk the extra mile and turn the other cheek. His followers are supposed to wash each other's feet, as Jesus did, because that's what Jesus' people do.

Yet I find it does me no good to wash someone's feet when I'm comparing their toe jam to mine. Well, technically, it does *some* good—I can get their feet clean. But the point of serving someone isn't to get their feet clean, it's to clean their feet.

It's easy to admire Jesus for habitually spending time with people of issue, including prostitutes, tax collectors and such. I often hear Christians rallying to a similar cry, "Let's be like Jesus and hang out with them and talk to them about God"—*them* being the sinners of our day. But does it bother you that if we went and hung out with *them*, we'd still see them as "them?" Does it bring you pause that it's so easy to differentiate between "us" and "them"?

Jesus said that judging assassinates the most important elements of belief in God: justice, mercy and faith.

Judgment kills justice because it elevates the judge's brand at the expense of another.

Judgment kills mercy because it leaves no room for grace and no hope of transformation. At best, it results only in pity.

Judgment kills faith because once the guilty verdict is passed, faith is unnecessary. Why trust in something beyond ourselves when we can be the standard by which others are measured?

What would it be like if we imitated how Jesus *didn't* see people? If we, like him, didn't see poor people, sick people, political people, business people, tax-collecting people, religious people or addicted people? If we didn't see people in their roles or their condition or lifestyle choices?

Judgment kills faith because once the guilty verdict is passed, faith is unnecessary.

What if we just saw people—period?

Perhaps, if we saw people as people, we might be able to rightly see ourselves.

I wanted to feel satisfied that evening on the bridge, but the thought of it made me feel as tacky as my now sea-breezed face and hands. I knew it was the wrong step to take. I hungered for a different satisfaction, one that doesn't judge others in situations like this. Though I'd not discovered it yet, I knew what to look for, and I wasn't going to stop until I found it.

That's who I want to be.

DISAMBIGUATION

CHAPTER 9

THE BIG IDEA:

Judging others sabotages our ability to be salt and light.

JUDGING IS PRIORITIZING SELF-INTEREST AT THE EXPENSE OF OTHERS.

It's sourced in our human (sin) nature and fed by our practically perfect, Outside-In approach. Judging results in giving ourselves the benefit of the doubt while taking it from others. We overlook or justify our own faults and simultaneously hyper-focus and condemn others for their faults.[61]

WE MUST COME TO TERMS WITH REALITY, WE'RE NO BETTER THAN THOSE WE JUDGE.

And we might even be worse.[62]

TO JUDGE IS TO BE A HYPOCRITE.

Being a judge means having the ability and authority to fairly evaluate and render a verdict. Since God is the only one capable of judging with perfect justice and righteousness, judging others means claiming a divine status that rightly belongs only to God. It is living a lie.[63]

WE CAN BECOME AWARE OF–AND AVOID–THE TEMPTATION TO JUDGE.

But it requires intentional effort. There are a great many things in this world that motivate us to judge and very few that encourage us not to. Maintaining a humble, beggar-mourner-meeker identity helps us see judgment for what it is.[64]

JUDGING CUTS OFF GRACE AND MERCY.

In contrast, choosing not to judge lets us see others as God sees them. We can offer grace and mercy to those who need it–and even to those who don't deserve it.[65]

CHOOSING NOT TO JUDGE OTHERS IS AN ACT OF FAITH.

Trusting that God will judge everything fully and righteously relieves us of the burden of doing so. Everyone–including us–will give an account of our lives before God. That includes forgiving others for not only their faults but even for the harm those faults have caused.[66]

Chapter Ten

Let Go

How have all the bad things people have done to you shaped how you see yourself?

CAN YOU IMAGINE a world without hurting? To have no knowledge that we could take advantage of or inflict pain on one another? To have no sense of vulnerability? To live free of being hurt?

Honestly, I can't. Hurting each other is all a part of who we are now.

But stories like Miss Henrietta's help me see this is not who we really want to be.

Ms. Henrietta Mildred is one of the kindest, classiest people I've ever met—though she would be uncomfortable hearing that. She has a smile that lights up the room. Every time I see her in her home church, she's dressed to the nines, hat and all. At 94 years old, she's seen a lot of the world, some of it good, much of it not.

Hurting each other is all a part of who we are now.

When she was a child living in Birmingham, Alabama, her dad was beaten to death by police officers on his way home from work. She lived with anger, bitterness and hatred over the event for years. It contributed to a long, dark season where she became an alcoholic and addicted to drugs.

Somewhere down that long road, she got to the end of herself and turned back to the core of her faith from her African American heritage. Jesus became a real person, not just a Bible story and a name sung in church hymns. She realized God's forgiveness for all of her own mistakes and wrong choices. Finding forgiveness for herself, she began to see her dad's murderers in a different light and eventually forgave them, too.

Now Ms. Henrietta says that she harbors no ill will toward them. Forgiving them was one of the final steps on her journey toward freedom. I imagine her smile wasn't quite as bright in those dark years. Now, living free and forgiven—as a forgiver—her smile is one of the first things you notice about her. The world would be a darker place without it.

How is it that the 94-year-old daughter of a black man beaten to death by white police officers at the height of racial tensions in the deep South can see forgiving her dad's murderers as one of the best choices she's ever made?

As noble and virtuous as this is, how is it even possible?

And what does it say to the rest of us?

Every week I log into my online accounting software as a part of managing my coaching business. I check accounts payable and receivable. I attach receipts and validate transactions. I send invoices. I reconcile the unreconciled. Everything is accounted for, kept in order.

It's what all businesses should do, right? With our business in order, we can report on profits and losses, confirm that more is coming in than going out, and balance assets and liabilities. After all, who wants to be unbalanced?

Keeping accounts is just what we do.

We take the same accounting approach to life and relationships. We tend to see things in terms of credits and debits, deposits and withdrawals.

When someone has done something wrong, they're expected to account for it. Payback. Eye for an eye. Even karma, some might say.

This is true for most areas of life, but it's especially true when it comes to personal offenses and forgiveness. We naturally take a transactional approach. You offend, I forgive. I give, you replace. I lend, and you repay (with interest, of course).

Unforgiveness demands an accounting.

They're all withdrawals and deposits recorded on a ledger. When the debits exceed the credits, the transaction's incomplete. Inequity remains, and the offending party is liable. Their credit score goes down, and they're designated as a risk for further loans until the inequity is resolved and a pattern of balanced behavior is demonstrated over time.

This is inescapably true, any credible audit will reveal it to be so.

From this accounting perspective, the concept of forgiveness is nonsense. The dictionary defines forgiveness as "to give up a claim of ownership or control, to grant a pardon, to cancel indebtedness or liability." How can we forgive the debt without some form of due repayment? Why would we?

Unforgiveness demands an accounting. Offenders have to "earn" forgiveness and settle accounts. If they haven't, they don't "deserve" to be forgiven. The ledger maintains a state of unforgiveness, and they're confined to a relational pseudo-purgatory until they can do penance and work off their debt.

When it comes to forgiveness, we're all accountants by nature.

When we walk in the doors of a restaurant, we become judges. Our patronage assigns us certain privileges, culminating in the accepted American practice of using our tip as a verdict. If the service is extraordinary and the food is exceptional and timely served, we tip generously. But if it's mediocre or worse, we reflect our assessment in a smaller tip.

This is typical and socially accepted. But in most cases, our judgment rarely takes into account the backstory—and anyone who's ever served in a restaurant will tell you there's frequently a backstory. We're at the end of a long process with many moving parts that all come together in the form of a delicious meal. But as customers, the back of the house isn't our concern. We think and act transactionally and make the judgment call that a tip is undeserved.

How is it that we deem someone "undeserving" of forgiveness? What makes it so?

There are times and situations when granting forgiveness is particularly daunting. Maybe it's when the offense has lasting consequences. Maybe the offender is already upside-down, a forgiveness credit risk. Often it comes when the offender was previously a close and trusted confidant or friend, and the offense feels more like betrayal.

I remember one man who talked about his adult son who'd left his wife and daughter to be with another woman. This man deeply loved his daughter-in-law and grandchild, and seeing their financial struggle and abandonment added personal shame to his son's actions. He finished off the story by saying, "I could never forgive him for that."

> Our reluctance isn't so much about forgiving the *offense* as it is about forgiving the *offender.*

There's a slippery slope in the justification we feel in holding on to unforgiveness in these cases. Our reluctance isn't so much about forgiving the *offense* as it is about forgiving the *offender*. Being offended by *that person* validates our right and authority to adjudicate. We feel authorized and commissioned, almost like getting a superhero power. Once we start down this slippery slope, it's hard to stop—and the descent quickly picks up momentum.

We've judged them to be unforgivable.

It's actually a version of the judgmental mindset we wrestled with in Chapter 9. It's subtle, and it seeps into the cracks of our character that we don't know are there. It prioritizes *our* interests over our *offender's* interests. It's the same co-dependent judging lover, whispering confirmations in our mind's ear that we're justified in placing our offender below us on the righteousness ladder.

Or, more accurately, that being offended elevates us a rung or two.

We have to be careful with this because it's so easy to oversimplify. On the one hand, we don't want to minimize or whitewash the offense and the real pain it caused. It's right to expect the offender to be held accountable. And, certainly, we don't want to paint the offended person as somehow being in the wrong, as if they bear the brunt of responsibility for the offense.

On the other hand, it's easy to take on the role of judge as the offended party. In this position, we dismiss concern for what's going on in the back of the house. We flush whatever backstory may have contributed to the offense—even though offenses frequently have a backstory. We focus our attention on the pain and disappointment we've encountered. We allow the offense to assign us certain privileges, culminating in the accepted practice of judging the offender as undeserving of forgiveness. And, by implication, *we* reserve the right to withhold it.

But consider what's behind claiming that right. In withholding forgiveness, we judge ourselves as sufficiently just and righteous enough to cast a guilty verdict according to a viable standard. How does being the offended party give us that ability?

As imperfect humans, the best possible judgment we can offer is relative. In other words, the only way our judgment could be fair and impartial is if we've never offended or caused harm to anyone else—which simply isn't the case. We've all been there and done that at some point.

The topic of forgiveness requires a breadth of wisdom and perspective. The red on the ledger is real. The offense is real, and everyone agrees an accounting is called for. It can't just be ignored, especially if the consequences of the offense are significant and lasting. And once the pain from the offense and the judgment of our offender get blended together, it's hard to separate them.

We must come to terms with the reality that we, as the offended party, are inadequate to judge our offenders as either deserving or undeserving of forgiveness. That's a role that only God can capably fill, and so that's a burden we don't need to carry—although, as targets of an offense, it seems right to do so.

This, of course, creates more questions than it answers. As the offended party, how will the offense be accounted for if I choose to forgive instead of judge? What's required of my offender? How do I guard against further offense? What practical steps are open to me going forward? And if I just let the offense go, what does that say about me?

As the forgiver, who am I?

Botham Jean was sitting on his couch in his apartment on a Thursday evening after work, eating a bowl of ice cream and watching TV. Botham and his siblings had emigrated to the U.S. from St. Lucia in the Caribbean. He was a graduate of Harding University and an accountant at PricewaterhouseCoopers.

Amber Guyger was Botham's neighbor, living directly below him in the same apartment complex. Amber was a five-year veteran of the Dallas Police and came home one night just before 10 p.m. after a long shift. Whether from fatigue or distraction, or both, she mistakenly went to Botham's apartment instead of her own.

When she found the front door ajar, she assumed someone had broken into her apartment, and her fight-or-flight instincts kicked into high gear. She chose to fight and entered the apartment alone (against police protocol) without calling for backup from headquarters two blocks away. Believing Botham to be an intruder and fearing for her life (as she later claimed), she shot him in the chest. Botham was unarmed—aside from his bowl of ice cream.

Guyger called 911 and stayed on the line for an agonizingly long six minutes until officers were able to arrive. During the call, she was clearly exasperated. As if trying to wrap her brain around what she'd just done, she stated 18 times, "I thought it was my apartment."

Botham died at the hospital.

Guyger was arrested and charged with murder a few days later, and a jury found her guilty.

During the sentencing, Botham's brother Brandt spoke directly to Amber, saying, "I don't want to say … for the hundredth time, how much you've taken from us. But I hope you go to God with all the guilt, and all the bad things you've done in the past. Each and every one of us has done something we're not supposed to do. If you truly are sorry, I know I can speak for myself, I forgive you. And if you go to God and ask him, he will forgive you … I love you just like anyone else … I personally want the best for you … I don't even want you to go to jail. I want the best for you because that's exactly what Botham would want … I think giving your life to Christ would be the best thing Botham would want you to do. Again, I love you, as a person. And I don't wish anything bad on you."

Then composing himself, he looked at the judge and asked, "Can I give her a hug, please? *Please*?"

The judge paused, then granted his request. Brandt stepped out from behind the witness chair and met Amber in front of the judge, who was wiping tears from her eyes. Brandt and Amber embraced for almost a full minute, talking to each other as sniffs and wailing broke out around the courtroom.

Amber was eventually sentenced to 10 years in prison.

Botham was posthumously awarded the honor of having a section of Lamar St.—where the police headquarters is located—renamed to Botham Jean Boulevard.

Brandt's very public forgiveness of Amber generated a spectrum of reactions. The incident was one of a string of events in 2018 involving white police officers using deadly force against black citizens. Some were concerned that Brandt's heartwarming gesture actually did more harm than good, creating a sentiment that we can just move on and not account for all the past offenses of police violence against blacks.

It's a legitimate question. Is forgiving our offenders letting them off the hook?

It seems like being the offended party leaves no good options. We can either hold on to unforgiveness and prioritize our interests over our offender's, or choose the cruel opposite, i.e., forgive and prioritize our offender's interests at the expense of our own.

The latter option adds insult to injury, dismissing the offense in favor of compassion for the offender. And if the offender is unrepentant or unremorseful, the insult is even greater. Letting offenders off the hook feels like evasion, not resolution.

All this leads to the question: How does forgiveness balance out the ledger?

It might help to realize that our forgiveness doesn't free *our offenders* from their guilt. Forgiveness *frees us* from carrying the pain and the hurt of the offense as well as the responsibility of trying to be someone we can't be, God. This is key because though we may have been the recipient of the offense, the offense is ultimately against God.

So forgiving our offender recognizes two things. First, that the offense was a sin against God and his creation. And second, ultimate forgiveness is available when they go to God and ask for it. This is where reconciliation ultimately occurs. So our forgiveness is, so to speak, forgiveness "on earth, as it is in heaven."

> Forgiveness doesn't free *our offenders* from their guilt. Forgiveness *frees us* from carrying the pain and the hurt of the offense.

The prospect we must come to terms with is a claim God makes of himself. There *is* a Ledger. There *is* an imminent capital-A Accounting, where all the debits and credits in human history will be brought into balance. Of course, the relevance of this is contingent on what we believe about God. If we don't believe this about God, then we'll struggle to let go of unforgiveness. But if we can accept that this promise of God will come to pass, we can defer our accounting to the One who can judge completely and justly.

Said another way, unforgiveness *demands* an accounting, but forgiveness *presumes* an accounting—the Great Accounting. This presumption is a step of faith, trusting that God will account for every wrong and redeem every bad thing.

I love to ride my bike. There's nothing like getting in the saddle, getting my heart rate up and cruising. The wind in my face and the pedal strokes in rhythm with my breathing clear the head and harmonize the soul.

I also love to hike. There's nothing like getting out on the trail, breathing in the fresh air and walking in and around mountains that both invite and intimidate. The connection with nature makes me feel significant and small—all at the same time.

I can plan out a bike ride, calculating how long it will take and the calories I'll burn. I can look at pictures of the ascent to Longs Peak in Rocky Mountain National Park, which at 14,259 feet is just a bit higher than my house in Florida at eight feet above sea level. I can logically wrap my mind around how challenging both riding and hiking Longs will be and the physical condition I'll need to be in.

But at some point, I have to get on the bike, and only then is the truth of my fitness level revealed. To climb Longs, I have to get on the trail and walk it out, which exposes my cardio conditioning for what it truly is, not what I *think* it is. Calculated fitness isn't the same as actual fitness.

In that sense, biking and hiking are truth-tellers.

Forgiveness is also a truth-teller. Lots of things get exposed when we face the prospect of forgiving someone else. It's one thing to understand it cognitively and another thing altogether to actually do it. Forgiveness isn't calculated, it's *practiced*. And who we really become fully revealed when we do.

For one, practicing forgiveness exposes what we think about ourselves. Being able to let go of unforgiveness comes from a posture of humility, where we choose to see ourselves as equals, not superiors. Forgiving doesn't put us *beneath* our offenders, it prevents us from putting ourselves *above* them. As C.S. Lewis said, "Humility isn't thinking less of yourself, but thinking of yourself less."

Practicing forgiveness also exposes our level of compassion. Though it can be hard to accept, our offenders are people, too—people who very likely have themselves been offended and then buried their hurt so they could keep moving forward. But pain eventually finds its way out, often in the form of hurtful actions against others. Understanding this backstory brings perspective and—if we allow it—space for compassion.

These steps of humility and compassion are, of course, entirely counterintuitive. It seems like a position of weakness, but it's actually a position of strength. It seems like a retreat into cowardice, but it's actually backing up to see the bigger picture. It feels like a passive step toward vulnerability, but it's not. It's an empowering, proactive step of courage.

Humility and compassion remove the indifference and cold-hearted judgment of unforgiveness, giving us the strength to release ourselves from what is, ironically, self-inflicted slavery to the ongoing pain and hurt of the offense. They catalyze forgiveness because, without them, forgiveness is just a theory. They break the cycle of hurt and allow peace to become a part of our identity.

We become peacemakers.

Forgiving is not about accounting, it's about identity. Are we willing to see ourselves as people who need to be forgiven? Because our opportunity to live in a state of being *forgiven* is directly related to our willingness to *forgive*. Forgiving and being forgiven are symbiotic. This is why Jesus taught his followers to include forgiveness in their prayers. "Forgive us our sins, as we forgive those who've sinned against us."

To ask God to forgive the mountains of all our debts and demerits without being willing to forgive others is a nonsensical, illegitimate request. If we won't grant forgiveness, how can we remotely understand what we are asking him for? Why would God support our hypocrisy?

By the same token, if we've received God's forgiveness but are unwilling to grant it to others, we devalue what we've received and misunderstand the grace by which it was given. Said another way, if we've held on to resentment, judgment and ill wishes, do we really want God to deal with us like we've dealt with our offenders? Of course not.

Jesus went on to say, "If you forgive other people when they sin against you, your heavenly Father will also forgive you. But if you do not forgive others, your heavenly father won't forgive you." This sounds ominous at first glance, almost like a threat. But we have to break it down in context to fully get its meaning.

Jesus is not speaking of forgiveness earned, as in God forgives us *when* we forgive others. Neither is he speaking of conditional forgiveness, as in God withholds forgiveness *until* we forgive others. Jesus is saying it's unrealistic to expect God to do what we're not willing to do. He's talking about forgiveness realized and received, living in a posture that's willing to forgive others for their shortcomings and faults.

It's a posture that seeks to be like him in image and likeness.

This is perhaps the most revealing thing about forgiveness. If we want to imitate God, we must practice forgiveness. Being unwilling to love our offenders enough to forgive them exposes what we believe about God's love for us. If we willingly hold on to unforgiveness, how can we grasp the unconditional love that God has for us? And if we claim to be oriented toward God but hold on to unforgiveness, how can we live out a loving identity as salt and light?

All this leads to perhaps the most thorny, scary and unspeakable aspect of forgiveness. Sometimes we have to forgive the most unforgivable, least-deserving of offenders.

Ourselves.

To be who we truly want to be, we *must* be able to forgive ourselves.

Self-compassion is often difficult. All of us—even the most unfeeling and narcissistic—carry some level of guilt for our offenses, and the larger the offense, the deeper the guilt. Though we rationalize it away or distract ourselves from thinking about it, it's still there.

Guilt is an icy companion. It visits and revisits us when we try to go to sleep—or go back to sleep.

Guilt is a prison. We never get out on good behavior. People can visit us, but we're always confined, separated from the real life beyond the fence.

But we can shed the guilt if we choose to. The same Great Accounting that reconciles our offender's guilt reconciles our own. When God forgives our debts, we are debt-free. There's no more red on the Ledger. Being free and forgiven is our identity. "When the Son has set you free," Jesus promised, "You are free indeed."

There's zero redemptive value in maintaining a low view of self. After all, we can't elevate others by shaming ourselves. This is humility, and it's just as necessary in forgiving ourselves as it is in forgiving others. C.S. Lewis' quote on humility—usually understood in the context of pride—is as equally valid in the context of self-compassion and shame. "Humility isn't thinking less of yourself, it's thinking of yourself less."

God intends for salt and light to be a part of our identity, to love those who need it most. It's part of Jesus' summary of the Old Testament: to love God with all your heart, soul, mind, and strength, and to love your neighbor as yourself. But consider this—how can we love our neighbor as ourselves if we continually shame ourselves as guilty and unforgivable?

Forgive yourself first, then, you'll be better equipped to forgive those who've offended you.

Wissam and his family are from Tel Keppe, Iraq. As a medical doctor, he was well-to-do by Iraqi standards. He had many of the things most people wanted—a nice home, cars, wealth, education and respect. He and his family were of Assyrian descent and a Christian heritage, though they maintained a secular lifestyle. They lived in peace.

Until one night in 2014, they didn't.

Tel Keppe is about eight miles from Mosul, where the Islamic State (ISIS) militants were headquartered. ISIS was a self-proclaimed quasi-state that viewed itself as having governing, religious, political and military authority over Muslims worldwide. This included the right to pillage, seize, enslave and execute anyone they deemed enemies of the Salafi jihadist branch of Sunni Islam.

On one of their rampages, they came through the town, commandeering all they wanted and killing whomever they pleased. The fact that Wissam and his family didn't actually practice their Christian faith heritage was an insignificant detail. ISIS saw them as infidels, at the top of the list of those deserving execution.

Wissam and his family escaped Tel Keppe in the middle of the night with nothing but the clothes on their backs. They eventually found themselves interned in a refugee camp in Erbil. Everything they owned was lost, and the life they'd known was stolen.

My friend, Keith, met Wissam at the refugee camp and relayed the experience to me. You'd expect to hear that Wissam was a man filled with anger, resentment and animosity toward those who took everything from him. But you'd be wrong. Keith saw a man filled with joy and hope. His smile and exuberance were a stark contrast to the crowded and desperate physical setting in the camp.

Wissam told Keith that during the experience, he faced a soul-defining choice. He could hold on to the hate and resentment and become a bitter and angry person, or he could let it all go. It led him to dust off the stories of Jesus from his heritage. Tradition and myth became alive and tangible. He found himself loved by God and forgiven, and Jesus' teachings gave him the model to forgive ISIS. In losing everything, Wissam realized that Jesus was all he ever needed.

"Forgiveness is stronger than hate."

Curiously, the faith ISIS tried to snuff out was actually awakened. Despite being confined in a refugee camp with no immediate prospects for his future, Wissam lived free and hopeful because he knew freedom had nothing to do with stuff and circumstances.

Keith watched it all in amazement. He saw the church that Wissam started in the camp, inviting the other refugees to join him on the journey of forgiveness. He saw news reports of Wissam's daughter, Manar, singing songs of forgiveness to the other refugees. He saw the evidence in Wissam that forgiveness isn't just rhetoric, it's freedom.

Wissam summed it all up to Keith by saying, "Forgiveness is stronger than hate."

On one level, hearing stories like Wissam's saddens me. It's a reminder that this world, while a beautiful and amazing existence, is not a peaceful place. For those who live in long seasons of hurt and the endless winter of offense, reading about the freedom and contentment of forgiveness is like imagining a tropical paradise they've never seen before. They live with the ache and isolation as constant companions.

Offending each other is so painful because we were never supposed to encounter it. The first humans lived without the knowledge of evil, without even the slightest awareness that they were vulnerable. Without sin in the world, there was no way to offend each other, so "They were naked and were not ashamed."

Imagine, if you can, a world where we won't need to protect ourselves from each other. Not easy, is it? Though it sounds naive and childish, this is the world we were created to experience. And it's the world we are promised to experience again, for all eternity.

Unfortunately, it's not the world we're currently living in. The great step of faith is to live now as if we're living in the world to come. "Your kingdom come, your will be done on earth as it is in heaven."

How is this possible?

This is the other level where stories like Wissam's encourage me, giving me hope and confidence. They reveal that we hold on to unforgiveness (in part) out of fear.

Think of unforgiveness as a learned process where an offense conditions us to respond with unforgiveness. The cancer of unforgiveness then metastasizes, infecting every part of our lives. It feeds the chaos of life and eventually reveals itself in jealousy, doubt, discontent, hatred, resentment, anger, bitterness and hopelessness—all driven from and incentivized by fear.

Inside this framework of fear, forgiveness seems like an admission of vulnerability. So we choose instead to hold on to unforgiveness, a kind of fig leaf we use to cover ourselves. We realize we're naked, and the accompanying vulnerability makes us uncomfortable. Ultimately, holding on to unforgiveness is a fearful position of weakness.

But if we replace the fear framework with faith, we can see forgiveness as a byproduct of something that's greater than anything we can conjure up from within ourselves. It's the fruit that comes from faith, the natural outcome of belief.

Forgiveness comes from a position of strength.

I forgive someone who's offended me because I want to focus on the condition of *my own* heart and not focus on the condition of *their* heart—which I have no control over, anyway. I forgive because I don't want to continue living with the pain, revisiting the hurt again and again.

I forgive so I don't have to continue playing the role of a judge—a role I'm incapable of playing to begin with. I forgive so I can live free, as a soul forgiven by God and able to forgive my offender in the same manner.

It might feel like forgiving our offender makes us more vulnerable, but that's just how it feels. I want to live fearless and unashamed.

Forgiveness is stronger than hate.

Forgiveness presumes a Great Accounting is coming—one that will reconcile every red entry on all our ledgers with God's. All the pain and hurt we experience will be compensated, invested or leveraged in ways only God can know. Those who forgive are freed from the prison of hate and resentment.

Forgiveness is redemption.

And those who've received forgiveness give it away most freely. After all, you can't give away what you don't have. Having received forgiveness, I see myself as valued and stable. Now I'm able to see others differently, too. Knowing who I am releases me from the need to be superior, to control or have authority over others.

Forgiveness is freedom.

Forgiving promotes peace. We become peacemakers, salt and light in a dark and bland world. It's impossible to love unconditionally and hold on to unforgiveness at the same time. If we really want to love those most important to us, we must begin by practicing forgiveness of those who've offended us—and often, these are the same people.

If we're holding on to what's behind us, how can we embrace what's in front of us?

Forgiveness is love.

If a Wissam can see that forgiveness is stronger than hate, why can't we?

If a Brandt can forgive an Amber because he believes in the Great Accounting to come, what do we believe in?

If a Ms. Henrietta Mildred can see forgiveness as the best choice she ever made, what does that say about the rest of us?

If we're holding on to what's behind us, how can we embrace what's in front of us?

We can't be who we want to be until we let go.

DISAMBIGUATION

CHAPTER 10

THE BIG IDEA:

Holding on to unforgiveness locks you in the past and reinforces everything you don't want to be.

HURTING ONE ANOTHER IS A PART OF WHO WE ARE BUT NOT A PART OF WHO WE WANT TO BE.

Though it's hard to conceive of this today, we were created to live without having any knowledge that offending each other was possible. We must come to terms with the reality that we're all offenders, albeit some worse than others.[67]

OUR NATURAL APPROACH TO FORGIVENESS IS ACCOUNTING-BASED.

We view an offense as a demerit, a debt that must be repaid or accounted for. Otherwise, the account is out of balance, unreconciled.[68]

UNFORGIVENESS IS A FORM OF JUDGMENT.

Though being the target of an offense makes this hard to accept, we are incapable of judging our offenders as undeserving of forgiveness. That's a role only God can play.[69]

HURT PEOPLE HURT PEOPLE.

Though it feels counterintuitive, having compassion for our offenders brings us freedom from our hurt–which in turn keeps us from hurting others. We can't have intimacy and peace while holding on to unforgiveness.[70]

UNFORGIVENESS *DEMANDS* AN ACCOUNTING, BUT FORGIVENESS *PRESUMES* AN ACCOUNTING.

While our offenses of each other happen at a human level, the guilt of those offenses is against God–and we must all face him at some point. Forgiving doesn't let our offender off the hook. It is an act of faith that God will ultimately account for all the wrongdoing in the world.[71]

THE TOPIC OF FORGIVENESS EXPOSES BOTH WHO WE ARE AND WHO WE WANT TO BE.

Forgiveness can't be intellectualized, it can only be practiced. When we do, we realize forgiveness comes from a posture of humility and compassion. We can embrace the reality that God is calling us to relate to our offenders in the same way he does.[72]

WE MUST BE WILLING TO FORGIVE OURSELVES.

The same Great Accounting that reconciles our offenders' guilt reconciles our own guilt.[73]

FORGIVENESS IS STRONGER THAN HATE.

God never intended for us to experience offense–which is why it hurts so much. But the thing that causes us all to offend each other will eventually be taken care of. This gives us the confidence to live out today what will be true in eternity. Where offense tears down, forgiveness redeems and restores.[74]

Chapter Eleven

Cultivate

Who are you apart from
your successes and failures?

ALL MY LIFE, it seems, I've tried to be significant and relevant. By this, I don't mean popularity or being some kind of hero. It's more of an urge to be real and tangible, to perform well in the roles I played and to make a palpable difference in the things that were important to me. I wanted to perform well and produce outcomes worthy of my effort and the respect of others.

I thought life was all about the fruit of my efforts. I strove for the significant act, producing the wonderful thing or the credible work. My habits, my family culture, the rewards and recognition from the world around me, the metrics I invented to measure my progress—they drove me toward equating myself with my life's outcomes, the fruit.

They drove me toward equating myself with my life's outcomes, the fruit.

The fruit was my identity.

Maybe that's why our attempts to landscape our yard were so frustrating. We had great plans for our yard when we bought our house (remember the sprinkler system?). I like a nice yard, but I don't know how to grow plants. I can kill any plant (except weeds) just by trying to care for it. So our master plan was a step of faith, albeit more so for the plants than for us.

The first thing I realized (as obvious as this may sound) is that maintaining plants takes some attention. After all, even a low-maintenance design needs fertilizing and occasional pruning. It takes attention, or maybe better said, it takes *intention*. Life doesn't just happen. It's not automatic, even when my sprinkler system is.

I like a nice yard, I really do. I could have artificial plants that look great and don't require any intention. They'd be easier to maintain. But they'd be … well, plastic.

A while back, my friend John invited me to a midweek men's gathering at his church, where we shared a meal and then watched a video of a well-known Christian author teaching on one of his recent books.

The video was a quality production, with multiple camera angles—including frequent crowd shots of smiling and engaged people. The lighting was subdued and warm. The backdrop was a painting of rolling Palestinian hills littered with grapevines. The stage props included lattice and greenery, and stage right, as if they were just left there by the harvesters, four large wicker baskets overflowing with grapes.

The presenter talked about the story of Jesus, describing himself as the vine and his followers as branches. He emphasized Jesus' point that the only way the life of a branch can be spiritually fruitful is by staying connected to the vine. Branches can't bear any fruit on their own.

Aptly using the stage-right baskets, he described four categories of branches: Fruit*less*, fruit*ful*, *more* fruitful and those bearing *much* fruit. He challenged his audience to reflect on the fruit of their lives—the outcomes from their choices, relationships, work, etc.—and then rate themselves as to which of the four categories they'd be in. The obvious point of the message is that God, the Vine Dresser, wants us in the fourth, much-fruit category.

After the video, we broke up into table groups for discussion.

"I haven't been making the kind of fruit God wants," one man said. "I know he's not happy with me."

Long pause.

"But this year's going to be different. I think my old issues are under control. They're behind me now." He could well have said this was the year he was going to hold back the tide or lasso the moon.

"Good for you. That's the attitude you 'gotta take," said one of his buddies.

"Absolutely," said another. "You can't let a bad year get you down. You have to get back in the game, back in the saddle."

The low-producing man spoke up again, "With God's help, right? I know I can't do it on my own."

"That's right," came the consensus encouragement, heads nodding all around.

It was the group's tone that struck me. Their encouragement was sincere but uncertain. It was as if they didn't really believe the advice they were giving but had no better options to offer. It had all the confidence of a roll of the dice.

I couldn't hold back any longer.

"I think this year can *definitely* be different for you," I said. "But I don't think Jesus is saying it's all about how much fruit *we* produce, through our own efforts. I don't think that's his point."

Another pause.

"I think Jesus is saying we need to stay connected to him. If that connection is real and strong, the fruit will come as a natural result."

"Oh, yeah. Of course," the low-producing man said.

"It's natural to want our lives to be fruitful," I continued, "and to measure ourselves by the fruit we produce. But the only way for a branch to produce *any* fruit, let alone *much* fruit, is to stay connected to the vine."

His look told me that nothing I said meshed with the other Christian messages he'd heard before. Neither did it mesh with his inner compulsion to perform well in order to gain God's favor.

It looked like he'd heard something too good to be true. It was too simplistic, like an adult nursery rhyme. He wanted to believe it but struggled to know what to do with his failure and guilt. It was the look of a man who knew something had to change, but he didn't know where to begin.

It was a look I'd seen before, so many times—on the face staring back at me in my mirror.

You can tell a fruit for what it is.

Oranges, for instance, all smell alike. Blindfolded and from across the table, you can pick up the unmistakable scent of a fresh orange being peeled. Though some are stronger and some are sweeter, oranges all smell alike.

Oranges look alike, too. Florida oranges (good for their juice) look similar to California navels (good for peeling and eating). They're different, but you know they're both oranges.

Oranges are like oranges, but they're not like apples, pears or nectarines. Oranges are oranges, every single one of them.

You can also tell a fruit for what it's not.

There's a difference between real fruit and plastic fruit, which you don't often see anymore. It sounds crazy now, but when I was a kid, lots of homes had a bowl of plastic fruit as a centerpiece on the dining room table. It was great looking, but everyone knew that everyone else's bowl was fake. Sort of a keeping-up-with-the-Jones'-fruit thing, I guess.

Both the real and the plastic fruit look like fruit and make for an attractive centerpiece. The real fruit is nutritional, the product of natural processes and intentional cultivation. The other fruit is only good as a centerpiece. It's manufactured. Plastic.

Both look like fruit, but one of them is pretending.

It was a sobering moment as a pastor when it hit me that the fruit of my ministry isn't my business, it's God's business.

It was an ownership thing. Like many pastors I've known, I'd dedicated my life in service to God, and I wanted to be a good model for spiritual best practices. It was easy to let my identity get wrapped up in church ministry metrics, like attendance, donations, staff size, the size of the church campus, etc. It's easy to let these ministry numbers dominate what we do and how we see ourselves. From time-to-time pastors see it happening. Every now and then, we talk about how stupid it is. But it's still there.

Like other professions, pastors attend conferences that promote popular keynote speakers. The best speakers usually have amazing ministry numbers. They're enviable numbers, even when you know it's not about the numbers.

I've gone back and forth on what to think about it. It's too simplistic to just ignore them. And numbers don't happen by accident. There are usually reasons the numbers are strong.

But I've been around enough to know that strong ministry numbers don't equate to a strong connection with God. It's possible to have impressive numbers while the rest of your life is a house of cards. A quick internet search will reveal a long list of church pastors (many with impressive numbers) who have been caught in scandals, abused women and power, and some who even recanted their faith and now preach against God.

> Strong ministry numbers don't equate to a strong connection with God.

It all raises an interesting question, how do you quantify or describe genuine connectedness with God? Jesus' illustration of the vine and the branches is pretty clear—he's the vine (our connection to God), and we're the branches that the fruit grows on (as long as we stay connected to the vine). So how do you measure your … branch-ness?

After all, quantifying fruit is easy. It's evident and available for everyone to see. But how do you encourage people to be a branch when all the metrics for branch-hood seem to look like fruit?

My goal as a writer was to get published. I thought it'd be straightforward, you know, like getting a degree by going to college. Put in the time, apply myself, gain some experience and batta-beem-batta-boom, I'm a published author! I was ready to work, and I expected the fruit of my efforts to just happen.

What I soon learned is the road to getting published isn't straight, and the way isn't forward. In the writing world, *being* published helps you *get* published. That sounds like something Yogi Berra would've said, doesn't it? It's the great catch-22 for aspiring writers seeking publication. So how do you *get* published in order to *be* published?

Well, one way is to spend hundreds of dollars to go to a writer's conference. My first stop is with a conference rep, a published author himself.

"You have an interesting idea," he says as he reviews my material, "and your proposal is put together well."

Pause ... wait for the 'But.'

"I like your style, and your illustrations are good. And I like the title, by the way."

"Oh, thanks."

Hmm, no 'But.'

"But,"

Crap... I knew it!

"As an unpublished author, your biggest challenge isn't the quality of your writing, it's your platform. It's very difficult to get published without a way to promote your book. Would the average book buyer know your name? Do you have any conference associations?"

"Well, I have some. But it's not like I'm Oprah."

"I understand. The best thing you can do is to work on your platform as you get to know different publishers. And have you talked to any agents yet?"

"No. You're my first interview."

"You'll want to do that. Literary agents have relationships with different publishing houses, so getting an agent to back your work is a great start."

So I make my way to the agent's table.

"Well, it sounds like a good idea—great title, by the way. I think you've really hit on a relevant topic. I'd be interested in partnering with you on this. But before I seriously consider representing you, you'll need to find a publishing house that's really interested in the idea."

Okay...

Then to an editor's table and wait for the appointed time slot.

"Hi there," she said.

"Hi!" I returned energetically.

"So tell me about your book idea."

"Well, it's about transformation, and how genuine change comes from the inside out, rather than outside in. I think change is more a matter of who we are than what we do, it's more about identity than activity."

"Okay ..." her response drifted off, and I knew I'd lost her at hello.

I chased. "That's why I titled it, *Are You Who You Want to Be?*"

"You might want to work on the title," came the dispassionate response.

"Oh, okay. I didn't ... I mean ... that's interesting because other people ..."

Ugh, this is going nowhere fast.

"...Well, can you tell me what would make the title stronger?"

"No."

"Would you like to take a look at the proposal and ..."

"No, I don't think so."

"Well, what would you do to move this project forward?"

"You should find an agent who can guide you through the process."

I wanted to say I'd found one, and he really *liked* my title.

"Yeah, I've been working on that. Do you have any agents you'd suggest?"

"No."

Okay, I think we're done.

"Well, uh ... thanks for your time. I hope the rest of the conference is productive for you."

"Thanks, you too," she said without looking up from her appointment book.

Let's go over this again, why, exactly, do you want to be a writer?

It's hard to explain the captivation that writing holds for me, which is lame since writers are supposed to be good at explaining things. It began in 1998. Well, actually, it began much earlier, in 1974, in Freshman English class at Catholic High School for Boys in Little Rock, Arkansas.

The class was taught by the principal, Father George Tribou, a gruff, uncompromising, cigar-smoking drill sergeant of a priest. One icon of his authority was The Boat Oar, his instrument of choice for administering discipline. It made a notable impression—on both the psyche and the backside.

"Bend over, son. And I don't want to see you in my office again."

Yeah, that makes two of us.

His menacing demeanor was surpassed only by his unfailing love and devotion to turning young boys into real men. I dare say he earned the respect of every one of his students who grew to manhood—mostly *after* they grew to manhood.

In front of the class, he said, "I think Damian is one of the most improved writers I've seen in a long time. Good work, son."

Like a typical adolescent, his comment didn't stick with me at the time. I ended up in engineering, a technical world of formulas and physical laws where writing is a muscle not often exercised. But when I switched to ministry, I was transported into a world of theology, philosophy and history. I read authors expressing abstract ideas about humanity and a God we can't see. It was the antithesis of formulas.

As a pastor with a young family and an old longing for significance, I began to journal. It was cool and oddly gratifying. I thought well of myself, believing I had taken a step toward profoundness. Then one day, I looked back on what I'd journaled and discovered a vomit of confusion, fear, gripes and ugly thoughts about the stuff of life. The catharsis was humiliating, and I realized if anyone else read it, they'd think me a miserable twit.

Embarrassed but repurposed, my journaling began to morph into writing. While journaling focused on what was happening in my life, writing forced me to go deeper to discover why things were happening. It turned me away from the effects and toward the cause. It became a search, like roots craning through crusty soil, scouring for moisture. Surprisingly, the search didn't uncover solutions as much as it uncovered new places to search. The deeper the roots went, the more nutrients they found. And the words on the page began to sweeten.

Even the process morphed. My journaling sessions felt good at the start but quickly became uninspiring. The writing was different. I often felt uninspired when I first sat down at the computer. I wrestled with ideas to get past the veneer of simplicity to unlock the truth, forcing words to align into meaningful prose. Finally, the words flowed, and I couldn't stop. I would write for hours, and the biggest impediments were my bladder and the numbness in my butt.

It became a search, like roots craning through crusty soil, scouring for moisture.

The writing effort reached critical mass one evening in 1998, sitting in bed reading Mike Yaconelli's *Dangerous Wonder*.

"I can write this," I blurted out to Cheryl.

"Why? He's already written that."

"No, not *this* book. My *own* book. I love the way he puts ideas into words, and how it moves you to action. I think I could write a book like this."

Then came those fateful words, "So, do it."

It's all her fault, this woman you gave me.

Looking back, Fr. Tribou's comment was prophetic. In a way he didn't anticipate—or maybe he did—he defined me.

He called me a writer.

I am a writer, whether I get published or not. I am a writer, regardless of what someone thinks of my book title. It's indescribably rewarding to know my writing has impacted another human being, to know I helped them wrestle with life in new ways. There's an odd sense of camaraderie with my readers, as if they've joined me in the search—our search.

Now that I've been published, I confess I like the sense of fulfillment. It's a wonderful feeling to hold my own book and see my craft come to life in printed and bound form. It's humbling to have a reader ask me to sign their copy, as somehow it makes it more meaningful for them.

As much as I've invested in the process, I know my part is actually small. The outcome of the writing process is the fruit of what God has done in me and through me. It's a partnership—I showed up and made myself available for God to put words to paper. My writing, his words.

The fruit is his, I'm just the delivery service.

I'm the branch.

I'm convinced it's right to *want* fruit and to do what it takes to *get* fruit. But I have to be careful because I don't ever want the product of my writing to become the reason I write in the first place. I don't want my platform to become more important than what I say from my platform. Instead of being a writer, I'd be a producer of books.

I don't want my platform to become more important than what I say from my platform.

If that happened, I think I would stop searching. My motives would get all out of whack, choking off inspiration. My writing would only be a regurgitation of what's already in my head—which sounds a lot like vomiting. It'd be unsustainable, like trying to produce a breath without first inhaling.

We have to be careful. It could happen …

It could happen to us, just like it happened to the Pharisees. Pharisaism codifies and manufactures spirituality. It promotes an impressive spiritual caramel coating on the outside, but on the inside, it knows no real intimacy with God. When it gets control, Pharisaism eventually dictates to God what fruit should look like.

Do we *really* think we can't fall into the same ditch? It's naïve to think we're immune from Pharisaical obsession with imitation fruit. To the Pharisees, life with God wasn't cultivated. It was manufactured.

Plastic.

We have to be careful, y'all.

Our old neighbors, Brad and Emily, had a tangerine tree in their yard. At certain points each year, they left grocery bags full of tangerines on porches throughout the neighborhood. They had to give away their fruit. Otherwise, it fell in their yard and rotted and attracted flies.

I still remember the day Brad delivered our first bag of tangerines, pulling his son in the wagon filled with their harvest. He mentioned what a shame it was to see good fruit go to waste, and he hoped we liked them.

Staring into the bag of fruit, a light bulb suddenly turned on—my identity wasn't the fruit of my efforts. Trying to be fruit or produce fruit apart from a source of life is nonsense. The fruit has no root. It's not pruned or fertilized. Fruit isn't alive. As soon as it's picked, it begins to decay. The fruit can't produce more and better fruit—unless it dies and is planted and then cultivated into a tree. The fruit is the good part, but it's only good for a short span of a single season. Fruit ripens, and if you don't give it away, it rots.

All those years of identifying myself by the fruit of my life came into focus. Even after I claimed Christianity, my fruit-first identity shifted slightly but not significantly. I was still trying to be the visible fruit of a Christian variety. To a degree, the way I practiced my faith even enabled my fruit-first approach. It wasn't an ego thing, it was more like a feedback mechanism. I was using the fruit of my life as confirmation that I was doing things right.

I needed the confirmation because the connection I had with God was, frankly, anemic. It was only as genuine as my identity allowed it to be. When a man sees himself as fruit, he looks dutiful and purposeful on the outside but unfulfilled and incomplete in his core.

Plastic.

That's what he sees on the face staring back at him in the mirror.

The question of how to measure vital and intimate connectedness to God nagged me for the longest time. How do you measure connectedness, if not by what we do, how we perform and what we produce?

I wondered if a branch could speak, would it be tempted to identify itself as fruit? Would its self-worth suffer because it is not used as a centerpiece or sold in stores? Would it long for the attention and admiration that fruit gets? Could it recognize that seeing itself as fruit makes every year a free-for-all, a chase for seasonal, ever-ripening production that ultimately separates itself from the tree anyway?

Or would it be content to see itself as the means through which the God of nature produces fruit—so that God gets the credit for it? Would it accept the tests of life that build up its strength, so it can support more fruit? Would it submit to the pruning of dead stems and new suckers that grow like mad but will never bear fruit?

If a branch sees itself as a branch, I like to think it would concentrate on the connection to the tree and nothing else.

If I saw myself as a branch, I would give the Gardener the right to grow me as he sees fit. What if he wants to produce fruit in my life that looks different from yours? What if he wants to produce sweeter grapes but less of them? And what if he wants a different variety of grapes this year from last? What if he's more concerned about how I fit in with the other branches in the orchard than about my individual rights as a branch? What if he's cutting me back this season so I'll be prepared for more fruit than I can imagine—several seasons from now?

If I saw myself as a branch, I would be present in this season of life. I wouldn't hold on to hurts or pain or strife in seasons past that have no bearing on the fruit he's trying to bear through me today. I'd realize that connecting to the past only interrupts the intimacy of my connection to the vine in this season.

If I believed I was a branch, I'd spend less time asking God to bring more fruit and more time tending my connection with him, so fruit just happens. I would value the perspective, counsel and wisdom of other branches who have different qualities than mine. Receiving feedback—though more admonishing than affirming—would hone my branching craft. I need it. I'd lean into these challenges to be a better branch, it'd help me become who I want to be.

If I saw myself as a branch, I would heed Jesus' words, "You can do nothing apart from me." I'd cultivate my connection to him and prune off the distractions like busyness, fear, jealousy and self-interest. Materialism, public approval, popularity, wealth … they'd all come off.

Then I'd be singularly focused on doing the things God is asking of me—instead of asking God to do things for me. "If you keep my commands, you will remain in my love," he has said. "My command is this: Love each other as I have loved you."

I'd be singularly focused on doing the things God is asking of me–instead of asking God to do things for me.

Only as a branch can I truly be salt and light, a preserver of life and a ray of hope to those in darkness.

Only as a branch will I reject the attempts at practical perfection that so relentlessly tempt me.

Only as a branch will I refuse the right to judge others and the hypocrisy of justifying my own faults.

Only as a branch can I forgive others who've harmed or hurt me in their struggle to be fruit—and not realizing they're actually made to be a branch.

Looking back, Jesus' call to follow him, love others and stay connected to him as the Vine was prophetic. In a way he obviously anticipated, he defined us.

He called us branches.

DISAMBIGUATION
CHAPTER 11

THE BIG IDEA:

We can do great things, but doing great things is not our identity. We are the means by which God's great love gets to others.

WE CAN'T MANUFACTURE THE SPIRITUAL FRUIT GOD INTENDS–ONLY GOD CAN.

A fruitful life is cultivated, not manufactured.[75]

WE MUST ADJUST HOW WE SEE AND APPRAISE OURSELVES, FROM OUR *PRODUCTIVITY* TO OUR *CONNECTEDNESS* TO GOD.

We were created to live and work in concert with God, doing amazing things out of an intimate connection with him.[76]

THE FRUIT OF OUR LIVES IS AN INDICATION OF THE QUALITY OF OUR LIFE WITH GOD.

A vital connection produces exceptional fruit in both quantity and quality. A weak connection can't and won't.[77]

WE AREN'T THE FRUIT OUR LIVES PRODUCE, WE'RE BRANCHES THROUGH WHICH GOD PRODUCES HIS FRUIT.

So any fruit our lives produce isn't ours, it's God's. We are just the delivery service that gets the fruit to others.[78]

TRYING TO MANUFACTURE FRUIT CAN DECEIVE US INTO THINKING WE'RE CONNECTED TO GOD WHEN WE AREN'T.

Being a branch requires a certain level of humility because branches don't chase for the recognition that fruit gets.[79]

CULTIVATING OUR "BRANCH" IDENTITY IS OFTEN UNPLEASANT AND CHALLENGING.

If we focus on being branches we accept that life's challenges are purposeful, whether or not we understand that purpose. Ultimately, being cultivated is a step of faith that God (as the Gardener) wants us to be more fruitful in ways we cannot realize.[80]

WE STAY ESTABLISHED IN OUR BRANCH IDENTITY BY LIVING OUT JESUS' COMMANDS AND LOVING ONE ANOTHER.

He set the example for us to follow. He then clarified who we are to be and what we are to do: As he loved all of mankind unconditionally, we are to love each other.[81]

PART 4

So . . . Now What?

Intake without output
is really just constipation.

Chapter Twelve

Weighing Anchor

How does who you want to be
compare with who you've been?

MY FIRST THOUGHT—probably offered out loud—was, "Man, that's big."

It was the anchor of the USS Arizona, on display at the entrance to the Arizona Memorial at Pearl Harbor. I couldn't help being forced into a reflective mood as I stared at the anchor, wondering how many seas it had sailed, what ports it had found and what stories it could tell of the boys who became sailors under her tours.

An anchor is an ironic memorabilia to display for a battleship. Battleships, after all, symbolize the power of a nation. They storm through angry oceans and unleash fury on their enemies. To do all of that, of course, the ship would have to "weigh anchor"—the nautical command for stowing the anchor in preparation to get underway. It saddens the soul that so capable a ship should be identified by the one part that restrains it.

"I wonder how heavy it is?" I found myself asking out loud again.

Probably more than you think (I thought, this time to myself). I guess it takes a lot to keep a ship from moving.

Getting into the memorial and looking down at the ship's size confirmed why the anchor was so big. Even submerged, the scale of a ship that large is hard to dismiss, it's like a city block that goes to sea. I should have expected it but didn't. I know there are bigger ships, but this was big enough to amaze me.

Exiting the memorial, I stood at the anchor again. It struck me how much smaller it seemed this time around. It's amazing that something so small can restrain so big a ship.

It's amazing that something so small can restrain so big a ship.

The ship is made for the sea.

The anchor keeps the ship—even the greatest, most powerful of ships—from going anywhere.

It's the same every time I get here. I've been breathing re-circulated rental car air since we left San Antonio nearly three hours ago. Now stopped, opening the door brings a rush of cedar and uncontaminated Texas Hill Country air that's a first breath at rebirth. It's omnipresent, the scent of fresh cedar.

My next awareness is the deafening quiet. No noise except the sounds of birds, grasshoppers and the wind coming up the canyon through the cedar and live oak.

And the spilling of water over rocks. My alarm clock at home drifts me to sleep to the sound of rushing water, digitally reproduced. It's nice, but it's fake. The natural sound has a unique effect over the course of a week. Night and day—all day, every day. It erodes the sharp edges of tension and anxiety. It forces me to take a deep breath.

And then another.

Cheryl and I have arrived with our young kids at the cabin on the Frio River near Leakey ("LAY-kee"), Texas, population 425. We come here almost every year for a week-long family reunion with Cheryl's parents, her brothers, and their kids. Leakey is some 3,000 feet above sea level and 150 crow-fly miles from the Mexican border. It's not on the way to anywhere.

The Frio is aptly named, running cold even under a July Southwest Texas sun. The cabin is the first property down from the Prade Ranch, where the Frio begins as water pouring 24/7 from a half-dozen springs right out of the limestone. The cabin sits on the west bank of the river, 100 or so yards up a gentle but rocky slope. Across the river stands a 70-foot canyon wall, shaped by centuries of gradual erosion and the occasional flash flood.

That deep-breath sensation is the same every time I come here. It's been this way for generations since a friend of my father-in-law's father discovered it nearly a century ago on a hunting trip with his buddies. It was this way 70 years before that, when John and Nancy Leakey were the first Anglo settlers in the valley in 1856, 20 years after the Texicans were sieged nearby at The Alamo. It was this way centuries before that when the native Indians made their still-visible markings on the canyon wall.

It's been this way for untold hundreds of years.

Things don't change much at Leakey.

Except, interestingly enough, the people who visit here.

All the kids are young adults now. They don't need to be accompanied to the river. They can make their own peanut butter and jelly sandwiches, and they don't ask you to read to them at night. Parents and grandparents have stiffer backs and thinner and grayer hair. I've changed career paths three times since I've been coming to Leakey. Two in our extended family have made their final journey to Leakey and have been spread here as ashes.

Sometimes we need to compare ourselves to something that doesn't change (like the river and canyon) in order to see the changes in us we don't often see. Change is an interesting, confounding experience, the only constant in life, so they say.

Change is inevitable, sometimes undesirable ... and often inconvenient. But I can think of some changes I'd embrace. There's the obvious winning-the-lottery thing. It'd be nice to have income instead of having to earn it.

I'd like some parts of my body to change. Some wish for tall, dark and handsome, but I'd settle for strong, lean and healthy. I resent constantly having to stretch and exercise—the required work to keep a physical condition in the later ages that my youth brought for free.

I'd like my speech patterns to change. *Strengths Finders 2.0* tells me I have a Connectedness profile, which means I see links between everything in life. I see connections and details in the same way that Haley Joel Osment saw dead people in the movie *Sixth Sense*. Turning it off takes effort. It's a challenge to explain things because I see all the connections as I talk, which makes me ramble and sound critical. I think I could live and work and influence my world a lot more effectively if I were a better communicator. I've talked to God about my speaking issues many times. He said not to worry about it, I wasn't the first person he'd worked with on communication issues.

I thought these things would change me, but God never took care of them. For a long time, I kept expecting him to, as if he were a maître d', a concierge that fixes issues and makes everything right. So I held on to them and waited.

On a recent trip where we spread my sister-in-law Carla's ashes, I remember looking at the canyon wall and realizing that I didn't want to end up at the end of my life simply being the sum of all my experiences and self-pursuits I thought were vital, but really weren't. The ones I believed were profoundly changing my identity but never moved the needle.

The unchanging permanence of the canyon reminded me that changes like that are situational variations in a short season of life, but they are not my life, they don't really define me. They're like the new shirt that eventually yellows in the armpits or the hit movie I saw last night that'll be yesterday's news when the next blockbuster comes out.

Outside-In.

There are, I'm coming to understand, changes God has in mind for me that are more vital. They are identity changes at a level that make the other changes irrelevant. Like contentment in place of wealth—not that wealth is wrong, but it's worthless without contentment. Or like patience and humility, or love or compassion that would be evident despite my stumbling speech. I'm aware of these changes in the quiet places, they're like whispers or longings or the wind coming up the canyon.

Coming to Leakey reveals something about the external changes I crave. Things that were priorities on a previous trip are distant memories on the present one. Stuff I was pursuing—and why I was pursuing them—have shifted. The timelessness of the canyon exposes the time-bound, fleeting pursuits I rely upon to measure who I am.

The canyon reveals that the changes I crave are urgent but not necessarily profound, timely but not eternal. Not that they're meaningless, they're just not meaningful. Sometimes they're big, but they get smaller after gazing at the canyon wall for a time.

The easiest way to reveal the temporary nature of things we think are important is to compare them to something that doesn't change. The unchanging wall is a reminder that cuts through life's noise like the whippoorwill's call cuts through the Hill Country night. The external, caramel-coated changes I pursue actually blind me from seeing the internal, core changes I long for. They're a preoccupation, distracting me from the opportunity for deep, vital change awaiting me.

The easiest way to reveal the temporary nature of things we think are important is to compare them to something that doesn't change.

The things I think will anchor my life can become a weight that keeps me from moving forward.

I know a woman who coaches business owners. She has a saying I wish I'd come up with, "If nothing changes, nothing changes."

My friend and fellow writer Marshele Carter Waddell tells a story about a waitress who came back to pick up the payment at the end of her meal.

"Do you need any change?" she asked.

Marshele paused, patted her mouth with her napkin and replied, "No, thank you. I've had enough."

Personally, after 60-plus years of seeking changes I wanted and resisting changes I didn't, I can relate. Can you? Change can be hard for some and easier for others. I was born at the tail-end of the Boomer Generation with parents who'd survived the Great Depression and World War II, so stability was an anchoring concept in life. Those in Gen Z (born after 1997) rely on fluidity, experimenting with everything from causes and roles to sexuality and gender to build their personal brand.

Many people look at the chasm separating these generational perspectives and say that people are vastly different. I disagree. I think all generations are a product of the societal events and culture that shaped their habits and perspectives. We, as humans, have not fundamentally changed. Our environment has dramatically changed, but we haven't. We still approach life with the same desire for fulfillment, in the hopes that what we do and how we do it will define us.

God wants to take us somewhere beyond the experiences of this world to a place we've never been before.

But identity is much deeper than the external things of life, like career, age, money, gender, sexuality, ethnicity, marital status, place of origin or the type of food we consume. We focus on these things with a Wizard-of-Oz-like expectation that our yellow brick road journey will take us to who we want to be. And when we get there, we won't thirst or want ever again.

There's something insidious about this temptation to arrive, considering that God wants to take us somewhere beyond the experiences of this world to a place we've never been before and can't get to on our own. It's like expecting the garnish to be the entrée, stopping at the chips and salsa that's only a setup for the whole enchilada. When God wants to give us the eternal kingdom, anchoring ourselves in the stuff of this world is settling for the shortchange.

I think of the story of Adam and Eve. They had everything humanity has ever wanted. But they bought into the lie that they weren't quite there yet, that there's one last step to the finish line, where they'd never be less-than again. It's fear-based, actually, sort of an identity FOMO. And living in fear is not living in peace.

So, Adam and Eve ate the fruit of a tree they shouldn't have, thinking they would arrive. Actually, they'd never left.

Until they did.

What we don't often consider is that God has created us with an identity in mind, an identity that's a unique reflection of himself. Yours is uniquely yours and different from everyone else's. This is what he offers to us, and he's committed to working a transformation process within us. It's a process that begins on the inside, then applies itself Inside-Out.

Our Outside-In pursuits—the things we think are identity anchors—are the dead weights that keep us from discovering the identity God has crafted for us. Since he designed it, only he can create it. He is guiding a change process in us, sovereignly creating opportunities for us to change and partnering with us to make it a reality. It takes courage because a change process we don't control can be scary.

We can hinder this change process, resist it. It's easy to get myopic about what we want God to do *for* us and, in turn, miss out on what God is trying to do *in* us.

So, it seems like the issue is not as simple as, can we embrace change (yes or no)? Instead, the issue is, are we willing to embrace change as an aspect of our identity transformation that will set us free?

That's where the true challenge lies.

Dominic was 28 years old and well on his way to a promising career as a consultant at a financial services firm. That was on the outside.

The inside of his life was a train wreck. He wrestled with guilt over personal failings and broken relationships. He had a daughter out of wedlock that he hadn't been a father to at all. He was angry and violent and drank way too much, resulting in multiple DUIs. He was addicted to pornography. It was all an intense path to self-destruction.

A coworker told him about Jesus and the opportunity for a new identity. He dismissed it at first but eventually couldn't deny his train wreck any longer and turned to follow Jesus. The first changes began in his heart. He started being concerned about others, especially those who were poor and underserved. He started living like a father, providing financially and being emotionally and physically present. Next, he turned away from his dependence on drugs and alcohol and after that, pornography. For the first time, he knew freedom from slavery to the things that had weighed him down.

These were big changes, but they were also the obvious ones. Other issues from his old identity had deeper roots and were harder to recognize, much less turn away from. He began to see things about himself he never saw before but realized he had to deal with. Anger, for example, took a full ten years to remove and replace with peace.

During this time, his career progressed. He'd become the sales side of a new software company that eventually went public. He walked away with a sizeable chunk of money. He'd started a well-intentioned practice of giving 20% of his income to charity after he decided to follow Jesus. But the practice had done little to prevent him from chasing success and achievement. On the outside, he was a churchgoing, Bible-teaching Christian, on the inside, he still worshipped the idols of financial status and accumulation.

Then, once again, everything changed.

He found himself in intensive care, suffering from Lyme disease. He'd lost 50 pounds. His fingernails had turned black, and his body was covered with red bumps that looked curiously like pencil erasers. The doctors had run out of options and suggested his family make end-of-life preparations.

As he lay there contemplating it all, he was convinced that God was getting his attention about the changes he was unwilling to acknowledge. That's when he got a phone call from a friend. "Dominic," he said, "this may sound crazy, but God just told me to tell you that he is going to heal you." Instantly, all the disease symptoms went away, his fingernails went back to normal and the pencil erasers disappeared.

You can call it what you will, but you'll never convince Dominic that it wasn't a miraculous intervention from God. He acknowledged the things he was holding on to and then promptly let them go. He now lives in a constant attitude of surrendering his entire life and living out the changes that come as a result.

Out of this attitude came more clarity from God in the use of his finances. Instead of fulfilling his pursuits of personal success, he saw opportunities to help others. He became concerned about people around the world being persecuted for their faith—many of whom live in desperate and life-threatening conditions. He wrote a book about it and then was instrumental in establishing the Alliance for Persecuted Christians, a collaborative effort that (among other things) recently helped save hundreds of thousands of people from starvation due to persecution.

Dom could have stopped at giving up alcohol or gaining freedom from pornography. He could have landed at giving 20% of his income away. He could have settled on gaining victory over anger. Any of these would have been wholesome and healthy. But stopping at any point along the way would have prevented him from continuing to be the person and fulfilling the purpose God intended for him. He would not have continued the journey of discovering what it truly means to be a child of God.

Battleships have anchors that keep them in place. We have things in our lives that do the same thing, despite the irony that we believe some of them are helping us discover our identity.

So what are our anchors, anyway?

Good question.

They could be anything. They could be secular or sacred. They could be old and familiar habits. They could be relationships. They could be attitudes. They may even be what you consider to be foundational beliefs. Chances are high that they involve one or more of the topics from Parts 2 and 3, like:

- Social acceptance, relevance, status or wealth
- The expectation of being satiated

- Self-determination
- The unwillingness to pursue God's intention for our lives
- A self-serving, practically perfect ethic
- Judging others
- Unforgiveness, resentment or holding grudges
- Identifying ourselves by our activity and productivity

Whatever our anchors are, it's easy to cling to them as if they hold some intrinsic value. We carry them around, expecting landfall and a respite from the fickleness and unpredictability of the journey.

But the anchors just get bigger and heavier over time and eventually become dead weights. They keep us from moving forward and create resistance to the changes God wants to make in us.

One of Jesus' promises that has been most meaningful to me is that if we genuinely seek after God, he will ensure that we find him. "Keep on seeking … Keep on knocking," Jesus says in one of his famous messages, The Sermon on the Mount. "For everyone who asks receives, the one who seeks finds, and to the one who knocks, the door will be opened." But in seeking something, I have to be willing to throw off the things that prevent me from finding it.

It's curious that Jesus' public ministry was immediately preceded by John the Baptist. John was a radical, a non-conformist and a prophet whose primary message was one of change. John announced the kingdom of God was at hand and that repentance was necessary to understand and be a part of this kingdom.

"Repent" is a term that has, unfortunately, become loaded with images of hellfire and judgment. Never was a word hijacked so unmercifully. To repent means to change—change your mind, change your direction, change your perspective, change your attitude. Change your dependencies and associations. Let go of one and take hold of another. Drop an old habit as you adopt a new and better one.

Change your identity.

Change.

We cannot go by staying. We can't transform by remaining. We can't realize our true identity (and all that comes with it) unless we decommit ourselves from the pursuits of our false identity (and all it comes with).

So, the real question is: Are you ready for change?

What if I told you that there's no way to discover your new identity without changing, without letting go of the old anchor(s)? Can you tell the difference between an anchor that keeps you from drifting and a dead weight that keeps you from moving forward?

Can you tell the difference between an anchor that keeps you from drifting and a dead weight that keeps you from moving forward?

If God were trying to speak to you about the difference between them, would you be willing to hear him out?

Because if nothing changes, nothing changes.

DISAMBIGUATION
CHAPTER 12

THE BIG IDEA:

We must willingly change–repent–
to experience our new identity.

WITHOUT REPENTANCE, WE REMAIN CHAINED TO OUR OLD IDENTITY AND THE LIFE THAT GOES WITH IT.

Old habits, knowledge and patterns must be rejected and replaced with ones that align with who we want to be.[82]

THE THINGS WE CONSIDER TO BE "ANCHORS" MAY ACTUALLY BE DEAD WEIGHTS THAT KEEP US FROM MOVING FORWARD.

It's easy to hold on tightly to certain beliefs, habits, patterns, etc., and not realize that the time has come to let them go. Even things that are good and wholesome can–not always, but can–sometimes limit our growth.[83]

THE CHANGE WE NEED IS TO STOP TRYING TO CREATE OUR OWN IDENTITY AND LET GOD GIVE US THE ONE HE DESIGNED FOR US.

Most everything we encounter in this world deceives us into thinking we can arrive at an identity of our design. In doing so, we block the changes God desires for us to align with his design for our identity.[84]

REPENTING MAY BEGIN AS A ONE-TIME DECISION BUT OFTEN MUST BE LIVED OUT OVER MULTIPLE SEASONS OF LIFE.

Living out repentance/change in this life can be difficult. But the more we do, the more we grow and mature in our understanding and wisdom.[85]

REPENTING–TURNING, CHANGING DIRECTION–IS A STEP OF FAITH.

It is grounded in the belief and trust that God is going to transform us into something we simply can't conceive of.[86]

Chapter Thirteen

Truth Is as Truth Does

What do you *really* believe,
and how do you know you *really* believe it?

So … IF CHANGE means letting go of the dead weight anchors, what do we take hold of in order to move forward?

What comes to mind when you hear the word "true"?

What do you think "truth" is?

What impressions do you have when you think about something that's "true"?

I asked a number of people on the streets of St. Petersburg these questions, and here's what they told me:

What comes to mind when you hear the word "true"?

"Truth is variable, by person. I think we all have a truth. I think truth is universal only when a lot of people agree on a given truth."

"Honesty."

"Truth seems to be an opinion, much less than like a universal truth."

"Realization."

"We have truths that we believe and then they're discredited down the road, or reimagined. So … yeah, I think truth is relative."

"Faith. Jesus."

"Facts. It's just the truth."

"I think ethics and morality, there's truth there, and that truth is … right. But it's still relative to culture and where we live. If we were to have evolved in some other place with different limitations, I think that truth would be different.

"Trustworthiness. Honor and integrity."

"Love."

"Genuine."

"God, as in 'I am the truth and the life.'"

"I think that actually what is more important [than knowing truth] is that we be good to people, and sometimes truth can be weaponized."

"Friendship. True friend."

"I've actually been thinking about this a lot, what is true? What is right? At the end of the day, we can all pursue what that is as long as we're good."

> "Your truth, or being true to yourself—following what your heart says."

> "Authenticity."

> "Honest, and real. Something I can trust."

> "Discomfort: In the sense that people are willing to speak the truth, and stand in the truth. People don't always want us to speak the truth."

> "Justice. I think it's because I'm traumatized by the context of my country (Columbia). So I think that when the truth comes to be known by people, justice is supposed to happen—I don't know if it will, but ..."

There are several things I noticed in asking around about truth. Almost everyone paused before answering, many said, "Hmm, that's a good question." I think it's a sign that truth is a bedrock concept—you can't go any deeper to define it, and you're left with trying to give an example of how it's applied and practiced.

I'm also struck by the irony that a concept seemingly as concrete as truth is such a slippery thing for us to define. Or maybe we've become *hesitant* to define truth, perhaps because many have "weaponized" it, as Tyler (one of the respondents above) so aptly stated. This all seems wrong, like we're overthinking it or trying too hard.

Maybe we've become *hesitant* to define truth, perhaps because many have "weaponized" it.

Another pattern I see is the one I find most curious: the widely accepted tendency to pursue and live out "our truth." The concept is that as we go through life, whatever perspective and experience we have at any given moment should be considered true, even though we know our perspectives are continually evolving.

I appreciate the intentions of this perspective, like accepting others as they are and valuing their individuality. I think it encourages humility and mutual acceptance, and the desire to be fully invested in the present. But that said, it leaves me in a quandary. If truth is only true to me and my experience, it feels like sailing with a compass that only points to myself. How should I trim my sails? Do I catch whatever wind is blowing the hardest? Should I be unconcerned about where that will take me?

Follow this line of thought. If our truth is true for us, then we don't have to be concerned for anyone else's truth—or their perspective of our truth. And if our truth changes at some point, that's okay … in fact, it's good because it's proof that we're growing.

So *my* truth is true for *me*. Which means *my* truth may differ from *your* truth.

And both can be true.

Or maybe neither is?

And that's okay … for each of us?

And what about truth for *all* of us?

And if all of our truths align today, what happens tomorrow when they don't?

If truth is only what you or I believe to be true, then *anything* can be true. But practically speaking, if anything is true, then *nothing* is true. And if nothing is true, how do we not end up in collective chaos? On what basis do we agree or relate or collaborate on anything?

If truth is only what you or I believe to be true, then *anything* can be true.

This all forces me toward a conclusion … well, actually, two conclusions:

1. Truth is either A) unimportant and irrelevant or B) it's absolutely important and entirely relevant. It can't be both.
2. Some things *have* to be false, so some things *have* to be true.

I've long believed that The Karate Kid is one of the greatest personal, learning, and development movies ever made ... albeit dated and cheesy. One of my favorite scenes is when Daniel is in the thick of his "training" and has spent many days washing and waxing cars, sanding wood decks and walkways, and painting fences and a house.

"Oh, miss a spot...," says Mr. Miyagi as he comes through the back gate carrying his fishing pole and his day's catch of fish.

"What spot? And, hey, why didn't you tell me you were going fishing?"

"You not here when I go."

Daniel fires back, "Well maybe I wanted to go, did you ever think of that?"

"You karate training," Miyagi retorts over his shoulder as he turns and walks toward the house.

"I'm what?!? I'm being your slave is what I'm being. Now we made a deal here!"

"So?"

"So you're supposed to teach and I'm supposed to learn, remember? For four days I've been bustin' my ass and haven't learned a damn thing."

"Ah," Miyagi dismisses, "You learn plenty."

Daniel sarcastically spews, "I learn plenty. I learned how to sand your decks, maybe. I waxed your car, paint your house, paint your fence, yeah I learned plenty."

"Oh, not everything is as seem."

"Oh bullshit, I'm goin' home, man." Daniel turns and begins to walk away.

You know where it goes from here. Miyagi challenges Daniel to stay for another lesson, asking him to recall specific motions from all his mindless washing/waxing/painting "training." Daniel, who thought he was doing menial tasks to earn his sensei's favor, was actually drilling his body. He was exercising new muscles and developing instinctive muscle memory.

When Miyagi asks Daniel to show him the motion for waxing the car, he follows it up with a sudden and violent punch toward Daniel's face. Without thinking, all the training kicked in. Daniel's hand immediately swings upward from his waist in a broad circle, instinctively blocking Miyagi's punch and redirecting it off to the right. A brief look of shock shows on Daniel's face, but it's only momentary as the next thrust from Miyagi comes from the other side, again aimed at Daniel's head. Daniel blocks the second punch, this time with his other hand. Miyagi then punches two more times with the same results.

Miyagi cycles through all the motions for each training task, then ends with a volley of punches and kicks. Daniel successfully blocks them all with defensive skills he didn't know he possessed, each as natural as taking a breath or blinking an eye.

Miyagi then stands erect, half-bows to Daniel and reminds him to always look his opponent in the eye. "Come back tomorrow," Miyagi invites before turning and walking into his house.

Some things that seem to be true aren't.

His mouth open in disbelief, Daniel looks around, first at his hands, then the floor and finally at his teacher walking away. *What just happened?*

Be careful with putting too much stake in what you perceive or assume to be real and true. Perception is personal and powerful, but sometimes we just don't see the whole picture.

Sadly, sometimes we see only what we want to see.

Tragically, sometimes we only see what we're told to see.

Some things that seem to be true aren't.

Not everything is as it seems.

When we think about knowledge, learning and assessing reality, we usually start with the brain. Our brains are amazing organs, containing some 100 billion neurons that each have about 1,000 connections to other neurons around them. The brain can process 11 million bits of information every second. It's estimated that the brain can store up to 1 petabyte of information—equivalent to over a thousand 1TB computer hard drives—all while using only about 10 watts of energy.

We've long assumed that the brain is the center of human thinking. But in recent years, scientists have discovered that other parts of our body are involved in learning and processing information. We now know there is a neural network surrounding our gut. It's called the Enteric Nervous System (ENS), part of the parasympathetic nervous system that oversees things like mood control, immune response, digestion and heart rate. The ENS contains an estimated 100-500 million neurons (three to five times the number in a rat's brain). Added to that is a smaller neural network around our hearts with about 40,000 neurons. Both these networks can "learn" independently from each other *and* from our brains, picking up on environmental cues and signals that our brains don't.

What's really interesting is that these networks don't just process information. In some cases, they *create* information—sending signals unconsciously *to* the brain. 90% of the signals in the vagus nerve go gut-to-head.

The ENS is highly involved in processing environmental threats and emotions like anxiety, nervousness and depression. The "butterflies" we sometimes feel in our stomach when we're excited or scared are the result of the ENS signaling to the body to divert blood away from the bowel and toward the muscles. 95% of the body's serotonin (a hormone that contributes to our feelings of contentment) is sourced from the ENS.

The heart, in addition to being a muscle, is also an endocrine gland. It releases peptides that help modulate blood pressure and improve kidney function. They also stimulate the pituitary gland to release oxytocin, often called "the love hormone." Oxytocin triggers the bond between a mother and her newborn infant, and both men and women have higher levels of oxytocin in the first stages of romantic attachment. It enhances many aspects of relationships and human interaction, including recognition, positive communication, relationship memories, loyalty, empathy, trust and sexual arousal.

Putting this all together, common sayings like "follow your heart" or "trust your gut" are more than just common sayings. They're describing how our bodies actually work. Our heart is taking the lead in discerning our environment and alerting the brain. Our gut is taking over some functions in the body before the brain is able to logically process any information.

Of course, I'm *not* implying that our emotions, feelings and experiences trump cognitive processes and logic. But I am saying that even the design of our bodies demonstrates how truth can exist beyond the limits of our framework for understanding and logic.

In other words, some things we think can't be true can be.

Here's another way to think about it. Imagine a large circle with a dot at the center of the circle. The dot is you, and the circle represents the limit of all that you understand. This circle includes both direct knowledge and conceptual thought.

But there is a limit. There are things outside our knowledge that haven't yet come into our circle. There are truths we'll simply never come to know in our lifetime.

We must consider that sometimes—not all the time, but sometimes—there are things we know to be true because they are discerned rather than learned. Sometimes our hearts and our guts process signals our brains don't detect. Sometimes we have a sense that something is right even when we can't explain why. Sometimes we have the impression that something's real even when its reality doesn't make logical sense.

Truth doesn't *always* have to be logical. Sometimes truth is illogical—and we just know it's true.

Not everything is as it seems.

When I go to the beach here in Florida, I usually stand where the waves wash on the shore. It's calming and soothing to have a warm Gulf wave lightly crash upon my feet, where the sand stirs up between my toes and the occasional shell topples across the top of my foot.

> There are truths we'll simply never come to know in our lifetime.

As the wave submits to gravity and returns to the ocean, it pulls the sand from underneath me. It tickles on the first few waves, but then it becomes uncomfortable as the pressure points underneath my feet change. The sand under my heels—where most of my weight is concentrated and where I need the greatest support—erodes fastest, and I lean forward to compensate for the toes-high posture. A few waves later, it becomes comical, and I struggle to avoid falling over.

I could just move to another patch of sand, but I'll soon be right back in the same situation. Or I could just choose to fall over, which doesn't seem like much of a choice.

I've tried it on other beaches in Texas and even black volcanic beaches in Hawaii. I get the same results every time. Sand is just sand, and it's not good for standing on when there are waves crashing around you.

If you want to stand firm, you need to be on something stable.

It's becoming popular to believe that what we experience in our *search* for truth actually *becomes* truth itself. The natural outcome of this approach is that we rely upon our environment to determine who we are.

In other words, we live Outside-In.

Collectively, this approach to truth has some interesting implications. On the positive side, initiatives like diversity, equity and inclusivity are championed. And there's a widespread sentiment to avoid judging others for their beliefs and perspectives (my point in Chapter 9).

But there are some predictable negative outcomes we have to come to terms with. One is that our individual truths are going to conflict at some point. Eventually, one group will claim the moral license to judge another group and enforce its social will by shaming, ostracizing or outright punishment—producing the very situation we're trying to avoid.

Another outcome is a higher level of social disintegration, where the increasingly individual focus creates a loss of connection with the whole. People become progressively isolated and unfulfilled in their search for things they can't define and won't be able to agree on anything because they believe in everything. Relationship bonds dissolve, and our tribal identity is lost. We will find ourselves collectively alone and isolated in the storm of a common existential angst.

You may think this is excessively pessimistic, but one could argue that the warning signs are already evident. GenZ—the group currently most invested in the "my truth" perspective—has the highest rates of anxiety, depression, hopelessness and suicidal thoughts of any generational group.[87] And it's getting worse. From 2007-2019, suicide rates among people aged 10-23 have increased almost 60%.[88]

It seems like this is more of a wisdom issue than anything else. I respect that some people are uncomfortable with the concept of ultimate truth, where some things are true and some are not. But without truth, we end up in a toes-high posture in life, compensating for our lack of balance and hoping we don't fall over. And when things get really bad, we just relocate to a different patch of sand.

We all have to believe in *something* because we can't live as if *nothing* is true.

I also respect the compassion behind not weaponizing truth and imposing personal beliefs on others. But what if, after falling over in the sand multiple times, I happen to find a patch of concrete where I can stand securely? Which is more compassionate, watching my fellow human beings fall over or inviting them to stand on the concrete with me?

It might be that *how we talk about* the ultimate truth is just as important as the truth itself.

In the end, we're all looking for truth—that secure place to stand, a foundation where we can build lives that won't collapse and fall over. So, the real question is, are we willing to embrace the reality that we all need to know what's universally true and that this truth is universally true for all of us?

After all, we can't *not* believe in something.

Said differently, we all have to believe in *something* because we can't live as if *nothing* is true.

I enjoy flying. I've always been fascinated with airplanes. As a former aerospace engineer, I know the technical reasons for how and why planes fly, probably more than the average passenger. I think my knowledge of flight makes it easier for me to get on an airplane than for some.

But regardless of how much we know or how easy it is to accept the truth that planes fly, at some point, we have to sit down, put our tray tables and seatbacks in the upright and locked position and fasten our seatbelts. At this point, we cross the line between knowledge and trust.

And only then can we fly.

From conversations I've had, it seems that those who dismiss the idea of an ultimate truth find the concept somehow … restrictive, like being forced to comply with something that will limit their freedom. To me, that seems like preferring to stand on the sand amidst the waves so that I can have the freedom to fall over. Which is more restrictive, being unable to stand up straight or having something stable to stand on?

I know this is a question each of us must answer on our own. I can't answer it for you, you can't answer it for others. But that we wrestle so much over this question breaks my heart—or maybe it's the neurons around my heart telling my brain there's some kind of tragedy happening.

It breaks my heart because I believe the controversy stems from a big lie that truth is some kind of conspiratorial trick to enslave you and make you less than you want to be. Personally, I was adrift at sea with no compass or rudder, subject to the prevailing winds and doldrums of my environment. The concept of an ultimate truth wasn't restrictive, it was liberating. Jesus' words have been transformational to me: "If you hold to my teaching … you will know the truth, and the truth will set you free."

It breaks my heart that so many who have claimed Christianity have overemphasized truth and underemphasized grace and compassion. When you're passionate about something, it's easy to let ownership of that belief become a judgmental hammer. Christians are not the only ones guilty of this, of course, but the reputation, unfortunately, gets tagged to all who would follow Jesus. It would be more productive to mimic Jesus' own approach of being "…full of grace and truth," as John the Apostle says in his gospel.

It breaks my heart that the false lie, so cleverly sown and deceitfully harvested, is so obvious and yet so hidden at the same time. It breaks my heart that it's now so socially polarizing we can't even talk about it anymore.

From where I stand, I don't own the truth, God does. But I can say I *know* the truth. Certainly not all of it, but enough to radically change my life.

And trusting it has freed me.

Our deepest trust is reserved for the things we know to be true. Will you, for example, fly on an airplane that you doubt has the ability to fly safely?

Likewise, trusting deepens our knowledge. You don't truly know what it means to fly until you put your trust in the plane, the pilot and all the systems that support air travel.

Trusting the truth is the key—not just comprehending the truth *intellectually*. Our knowledge is only theory until we actually trust it. Like Neo choosing Morpheus' red pill in *The Matrix*, trusting is seeing the truth for ourselves as it is lived out.

Truth is as truth does.

Trust catalyzes truth, making it part of our identity. Truth is a source of life, and then it becomes a part of life. Truth isn't just an intellectual factoid, a positional argument or a technical talking point. Trust is the fruit of a life firmly planted in the soil of truth.

Trusting the truth helps us to stop looking for another patch of sand. We stop compensating, and we give up coping.

And we can be, finally, free.

DISAMBIGUATION
CHAPTER 13

THE BIG IDEA:

To profoundly change,
we must accept and trust in that which is true.

SOME THINGS MUST BE FALSE, SO SOME THINGS MUST BE TRUE.

Everything isn't true, only truth is true.[89]

SOME THINGS THAT SEEM TO BE TRUE AREN'T.

Truth isn't just what we happen to perceive at the moment.[90]

SOME THINGS WE THINK CAN'T BE TRUE CAN BE.

We tend to limit truth to those things we've experienced, or that fit our logic framework. But some things are true that we don't–or can't–understand.[91]

WE HAVE TO BELIEVE IN SOMETHING BECAUSE WE CAN'T LIVE AS IF NOTHING IS TRUE.

Living as if nothing is true (or as if everything is true) may be convenient, but is actually practical foolishness.[92]

TRUST CATALYZES TRUTH INTO FAITH, WHERE IT BECOMES PART OF OUR IDENTITY.

Knowing that the truth is true isn't the key, *trusting* the truth is. Faith/belief is complete and ongoing trust that the object of our faith is true, without having physical evidence or the ability to control our circumstances.[93]

Chapter Fourteen

Practice, and Making Perfect

If you're on the road to becoming who you want to be, what will you do–and how will you do it?

"HEY, NATHAN! HOW's it going?"

"Good, man. How about you?"

My first coaching session with Nathan.

"I'm doing well. I'm looking forward to our conversation."

"Yeah, me too."

"So, tell me what's on your mind. What challenge or issue would you like to discuss?"

"Well, I'm good, you know? Doing pretty well."

"Cool. So tell me more about what's going well."

"Well, everything, really. I'm making good progress. If I could just not be so busy, that'd be nice."

"OK, good. What would you say is working best at the moment?"

"Well, people are excited about church."

Nathan was a pastor of a new church startup. The church was less than a year old, and things were still in flux. He'd approached me about coaching him in his role as the congregation's leader.

"Great. What are they most excited about?"

"Well, I think we've got a new expression of church. We make it easy for people to come to church—and in many cases come *back* to church. We speak their language, you know? So many people reject church because they don't think it's relevant. And so many others left church because it made them feel guilty for who they were not. But we don't do that. We want them to feel welcomed and valued. You know, God loves you just as you are."

I'm starting to get the impression Nathan has practiced these lines before, like from the About Us *page on their website ...*

"Sounds like people have been responding to that, huh?"

"Oh yeah, for sure! I had a guy come up to me after the service the other day and thank me. He said he'd never thought he'd spend his Sunday mornings going to church. He was so glad his girlfriend forced him to come."

"I can tell that was rewarding for you. So what do you need to do moving forward to lead this young church?"

"Well, I think just keep doing what I'm doing. You know, God does it all, you just have to get out of the way."

"So, how satisfied are you with where you're at?"

"Well, I'm the type of guy that's never satisfied—always hungry, you know? There's always more you can do. We're not perfect, after all, only God is perfect."

"Yeah, I think that's true. So if there were an area in particular that you aren't satisfied with, what would it be?"

"I think it would be giving myself enough credit. It's sort of a thankless job to lead a church. There's always more to do than time to do it. And we work with volunteers, not paid staff. I've been at this long enough to know that you can't beat yourself up when things don't go perfectly. It's *so* easy to get discouraged and put pressure on yourself. But you just can't."

"So what could you do to give yourself more credit?"

"Nothing, you know? The credit all goes to God. He's allowed us to be successful. It's enough for me to know that we're doing what he wants us to do."

And on it went for 20 minutes. Nathan wanted coaching to improve his leadership skills, but our conversation was going nowhere. The more questions I asked, the more tentative he became. My first coaching session with Nathan didn't go well for a couple of reasons. For one, I was a relatively new coach, still honing the skills of creating a context for coaching and getting past the initial vulnerability barrier. The other was that Nathan simply wasn't ready for coaching.

When you can't step forward, you either don't trust what you're stepping into, or you simply don't want to change. Or both.

He'd said he understood how coaching worked, but coaching was *not* working for him. He'd said he wanted to get better as a leader, but the effort he was expending toward *not* answering the questions told me he wasn't ready.

When you can't step forward, you either don't trust what you're stepping into, or you simply don't want to change.

Or both.

Her name was Angela. We were working in our front yard and saw her ambling by herself in the middle of the street. To say she was irate (and high on something) was an understatement. She was cussing and angry, throwing out accusations and threats as if she was talking to someone next to her.

"Are you alright?" Cheryl asked her as she got within earshot.

She shot back defensively, "What's the matter, don't I look alright?"

"Well, no, you look upset."

She then went into a tirade about someone stealing her money, life not being fair, people who were out to get her and a handful of other rapid-fire, profanity-laced overtures about how sucky life was. We eventually calmed her down enough to have a conversation. We found out that she was new in town, trying to find a job to get some money so she could get back to her daughter and be a real mom. She, like so many others, had fallen on hard times.

To avoid being homeless, she got a room with a local slum lord who gives homeless people free housing and $20 a day to work in his real estate "business." It's just enough money to get some convenience store food and keep an addictive habit, but not enough to make life work.

Eventually, the conversation turned to spiritual matters. I asked her, "What comes to mind when I say the name 'Jesus?'"

"Oh, I know the Man upstairs. I talk to God all the time."

She went on to talk about going to church as a kid and her mom having a Bible. But nothing she said gave us the impression she had any tangible connection with God today.

"Does he ever talk to you?" I asked.

"No," came her confused and terse reply, like I'd asked her if the moon was really made of cheese.

"Are you sure? What if he's trying to say something to you and you just haven't heard him?"

There was a long pause as she fought through the intoxication and anger to consider the possibility. Her face brightened a bit, a flash of hope that looked beyond her circumstances to a different life. But it suddenly evaporated, and her anger and hopelessness returned. "I'm gonna get my money back," she promised as she ambled away from what had become an uncomfortable conversation. "I know who took it, and they're gonna pay for it!"

Angela's story stuck with me for a long time. She defaulted to the faith practices of her childhood to validate her current relationship with "the man upstairs." It's made me wonder about those who believe in God or a higher power. Why do we practice what we practice, and what value does it bring? And, perhaps most importantly, what does God think of it?

A perspective that has been reorienting for me comes out of the gospel of Luke. Jesus says, "Why do you call me 'Lord,' and not do what I say?" Jesus' rhetorical question brings great clarity, revealing four possible faith practice scenarios.

The first is that we don't do what he says because we don't believe him to be God (even though we might claim to).

A second would be that we believe him to be God, but we don't hear him (whether we're trying to hear him but can't or we're not trying to hear him at all).

A third scenario is that we believe him to be God, and we hear him, but we dismiss what he says and do our own thing instead.

The fourth scenario is dramatically different from the others. We believe him to be God, we hear him and we respond to his words and put them into practice.

If we believe that God exists and can be personally interacted with, only the last scenario makes sense, right? Why would we practice our faith in any other way than to be receptive to God and align ourselves with him?

The practice of our faith indicates the substance of our faith.

The practice of our faith indicates the substance of our faith. We can go to church or follow a religious tradition without actually trusting in anything or changing who we are. Is it faith we're practicing? Or is it something else? And how can we know the difference?

Like Nathan in the coaching story, we can say we want to move forward and be devoted to our beliefs, but when it comes down to it, we either don't trust what we're stepping into or we simply don't want to change.

Or both.

In certain parts of the world today, being a Christian isn't a preferential choice. It's a potential life-and-death decision. It was the same in the early years of Christianity in the Roman Empire. It began with Nero, who blamed the A.D. 64 fire in Rome on Christians. He had them fed to the lions for sport in the Coliseum, doused in oil and set ablaze—alive—to light the streets of Rome at night.

The persecution became widespread in the last half of the third century under Decius, Valerian and Diocletian. They saw this new and growing religion as a departure from historical Roman culture. They wanted to return Rome to its glory years and reestablish its social and cultural roots, and getting rid of Christianity seemed to be low-hanging fruit.

Systematic, empire-wide persecution was instituted. High-ranking church leaders were killed. Christians were rounded up and forced to publicly offer a sacrifice to the gods. Many professing Christians recanted their faith, while those who held true either went into hiding or were martyred. Christian senators—an indication that the faith had spread even to the upper and ruling classes by this time—were stripped of their titles and property, followed by execution if they didn't offer the sacrifices.

Diocletian's persecution was the most severe. He purged the army of Christians, destroyed houses of worship, prohibited public worship gatherings, burned copies of scriptures and re-enslaved Christians who had been freed. Following Nero's example, many were burned alive.

It's a curious, historical fact that Christianity as a movement has grown fastest, and its members have been most dedicated during times of persecution—a fact that remains true even today. And, by contrast, in times where it's been privileged, authorized and established, it has become institutional, materialistic and politically aligned. The convenience of faith, it seems, hasn't inspired the genuine practice of it. Convenience doesn't call us to change or trust much.

What faith would you "practice" if you knew that attending a gathering or wearing a cross necklace would make you a target for being arrested and having your bank accounts seized? What would you say if someone held a gun to your head and told you to recant your faith or die?

These are sobering questions, made even more sobering when considering that confusion or reluctance to answer questions like these might indicate that you either don't trust what you're stepping into or you simply don't want to change.

Or both.

Years have four seasons—except in Florida, where there are really only two, Hot and Pleasant. At the end of Pleasant (when most places are enduring winter), all the oak trees suddenly realize A) it's the beginning (not the end) of Hot, and B) there won't be a Fall. So, they cram Fall and Spring activities into a few weeks, dropping their leaves and pollinating all at once. If you have any allergies to oak, late February and March are *not* good months to visit Florida.

Life has seasons. They usually don't follow a calendar, but when you reach the end of a season, you somehow get perspective, you know another one's coming.

It was at the end of one of life's seasons that I came to realize I couldn't make myself complete, no matter how hard I tried—or how hard I tried to ignore it. I'd been trying to be whole by doing the right thing. My attempts at *doing* good couldn't resolve the guilt I had over not *being* good. I had no more backyard left to bury my guilt.

My attempts at *doing* good couldn't resolve the guilt I had over not *being* good.

So I chose to stop digging and follow Jesus instead.

At the end of another season, I realized my well-intentioned and positive faith practice was … incomplete. I was at peace about the afterlife but not at peace with the present life. I was fatigued with the stress. I didn't want to be afraid anymore. Or tired. Irritable. Jealous. Judgmental. To live for the approval of others.

Anymore.

The search for this peace revealed something I'd not seen previously, i.e., a continual pattern of trying to build my identity from the Outside-In. Once I saw it, I couldn't unsee it.

So I gave up, or actually … surrendered.

This step of surrender turned out to be a season in itself, a series of experiences and a perspective that became progressively definable.

The more I practiced surrender, the more I saw that remained unsurrendered—the parts of my old identity I don't easily give up.

I realized that to get to surrender, you have to put change (repenting) and trust (belief in what's true) into practice. A word the Bible frequently uses for practice is "obey"—a word which, unfortunately, carries a lot of negative connotations in our modern context. There are two Greek words that are frequently translated as "obey," and understanding them makes the concept of obedience more bearable. One (*tereo*) focuses on our actions. It means to keep an eye on, to watch, or to guard. The other (*hupakoen*) focuses on our posture. It describes being in a state of actively hearing, like a doorkeeper who is listening and prepared to open the door when someone approaches.

Without practice, trust is nothing more than intellectual activity, and change is staying put while keeping your options open.

Taken together, the practice—or obedience—of trust and change is the essence of living in a new identity. Without practice, trust is nothing more than intellectual activity, and change is staying put while keeping your options open.

Nothing happens without practice.

Admittedly, it can be kind of scary when you realize the Outside-In approach to identity is like a sinking ship, and the lifeboat is this thing called Inside-Out that you've never used before. But not choosing the Inside-Out lifeboat is actually a choice for the sinking ship of Outside-In, though it feels like indecision. And no one is going to force you to practice your identity Inside-Out—including God.

For me, practicing what I believe to be true means putting all my chips on the table. It means living in an uncompromised state. It means clarity—not necessarily black and white, but being confident in my convictions and values. It means walking my talk and being non-hypocritical. Stable yet peaceful.

This all-in approach forces me to put into practice what I believe, not just conceive or give mental assent to a set of theological propositions. Everyone has to make this choice based on the content of their faith, but for me, it focuses most clearly on what I believe about Jesus and acting on a simple choice: Follow him or not.

The Bible says that Jesus became human through miraculous means, being conceived and carried in the uterus of a woman who'd never had sex. He performed miraculous acts no human ever had—not tricks or illusions but miracles of healing and even raising dead people back to life.

At his death, according to ancient Jewish ceremonial custom, he became the spotless lamb that was payment for our sins. Then he became the high priest who presented the blood of the sacrifice to God. It was the perfect fulfillment of the requirements of the Jewish law, once and for all so that no more sacrifices are needed.

Then, three days later, he came back to life, ending all doubt about the claims of his identity as God's son. He now offers that same relationship to us—if we choose to follow him. His life is the model for our new identity.

These details are sufficiently substantiated to allow me to believe him. So it gets my attention when Jesus says, "Anyone who hears my words and acts on them is wise, like a person who builds a house on solid rock."

Why would the wise man build his house on a rock? Lucky choice? Hardly. Ever tried to dig through rocky soil to put down a foundation? The sandy Florida soil makes it easy to dig a foundation, but it couldn't hold up to Hurricane Ian, which reshaped the barrier island of Captiva in 2022. The wise man had probably built a previous house on sand and watched it collapse, or he knew someone who did.

Those who build their house on a rock *choose* that plot of land. They choose permanence and discipline over expediency. They know the truth that rock is a better foundation for a house. They are committed to the task of personal change and have experienced its fruit in their life, so they're willing to invest the extra time and energy it takes to put it into practice.

They have become wise.

The issue of identity is ultimately a *wisdom* issue.

The issue of identity is ultimately a *wisdom* issue. We can choose to continue practicing either an Outside-In, human-driven approach to life that will never perfect us at our core. Or we can begin practicing an Inside-Out, God-designed approach that will be the foundation for everything we are and do in life.

Or, borrowing from Yoda to make it plainer, do … or do not. There is no *try*.

Do you want to build your identity on something that will erode and crash? Or do you want to build it on something that will stand the test of time?

That decision—and the way you put it into practice—is yours to make.

DISAMBIGUATION

CHAPTER 14

THE BIG IDEA:

We can't be who we want to be without putting our new identity into practice.

UNWILLINGNESS TO PRACTICE A NEW IDENTITY POINTS TO EITHER A LACK OF TRUST OR A REFUSAL TO CHANGE—OR BOTH.

If you find yourself stuck, repeatedly dealing with the same issues, fears, anxieties, etc., it might be that there's something about the way forward that you don't trust and/or that there's something about your current state that you want to hold on to.[94]

THE WAY WE PRACTICE OUR FAITH REVEALS THE SUBSTANCE OF OUR FAITH.

"Practicing" faith is more than just participating in activities, rituals and customs. Practice requires engaging faith in real-life situations where faith is the only thing that gets us through it.[95]

WE EITHER BELIEVE AND CHANGE, OR WE DON'T BELIEVE AND STAY THE SAME.

We can't be in two places at the same time. We must either be who we want to be or be who we've always been. Our response to life's challenges and opportunities reveals which identity we're practicing.[96]

CHOOSING NOT TO PRACTICE YOUR NEW IDENTITY IS ACTUALLY A CHOICE TO KEEP YOUR OLD ONE.

Practice (obeying) is living out your belief (trust) and your internal changes (repentance). If you believe your identity is new, but you're not practicing it, do you really trust it ... and has your identity really changed?[97]

IDENTITY COMES DOWN TO A WISDOM DECISION, PRACTICE IT OR NOT.

As Yoda said: There is no try.[98]

PART 5

Putting It Into Perspective

At some point, you really have to consider the "why" of it all for things to truly make sense.

Chapter Fifteen

Getting the Big Picture

If you had to explain to someone else
how to find your true identity,
what would you say?

AN ABSTRACT, PHILOSOPHICAL topic like identity can be complicated and nebulous. It's hard to define. With no mass or height or wavelength, it can't be measured. Where does identity begin, and things like IQ or personality end?

I feel the need to apply one of my favorite quotes from Albert Einstein: "Everything must be made as simple as possible. But not simpler." I want to lay out clearly the process of identity change. You may sense a change in style as I shift from narrative to informative content. Hopefully, the additional clarity will offset the change in the reading experience.

What is identity, anyway?

There are common associations with the word "identity" that need to be stripped away. Your identity is not your personality or your Enneagram type. It's not your IQ or intellectual content, or education level. It's not your ethnicity. It's not your age or generational grouping. It's not your country of origin. It's not your hobby. It's not your physical characteristics and how tall, short, thick or thin you might be. Identity is not the roles you play, or the accomplishments and failures you've had in those roles. It's not your vocation. It's not the category of food you consume or can't consume. It's not the habits you've picked up or the things you might be addicted to. It's not your marital status. It isn't your gender. It's not your sexual preference. It's not your political affiliation or your housing status. It's not your perspective on faith or your religious heritage. It's not the family you were brought up in or ran away from. It's not your social class or net worth. It's not the disease you're fighting. It's not what you're afraid of or anxious about.

Your identity is not related to the environment around you.

Your identity isn't any kind of label.

Identity is much deeper, it's more basic and foundational than all these.

Who you are at a soul level, without qualifiers or descriptors.

Simply stated, your identity is your self-conception at the level where you can be known, the awareness of self as embodied consciousness.[99] It's who you are at a soul level, without qualifiers or descriptors. It's who you are as a unique and viable individual, distinct from everyone else. It's the level at which God sees and knows you.[100]

Your identity is … *you.*

Who "you" are is deeper and more fundamental—more existential—than all the things we typically use to discuss identity and classify ourselves. Accepting this truth is absolutely critical to the discovery process. Because if we don't, we'll always hold on to an old and inferior identity that is nothing but a lie and an anchor, a dead weight that prevents us from seeing ourselves as we really are—and really can be.

There's a second aspect to identity that must also be grasped. Who "you" are is not fixed, but rather is in a constant state of formation.

Technically, philosophy and psychology have recently begun to refer to this view of identity as *narrative* identity. It's classified as "narrative" because our self-conception is a story in process. Dr. Dan P. McAdams, Professor of Human Development and Social Policy at Northwestern University, defines narrative identity as "a life story—an internalized narrative integration of past, present, and anticipated future which provides lives with a sense of unity and purpose."[101]

He goes on to describe it this way:

> "Narrative identity is a special kind of story—a story about how I came to be the person I am becoming ... A person's story, thus, explains how he or she continues to affirm a sense of 'inner sameness and continuity' across different situational and role contexts. The life story also integrates life in a [historical] sense ... showing how the self of yesterday has become the self of today, the very same self that hopes or expects to become a certain kind of (different but still similar) self in the future."[102]

In describing how he formed his hypothesis about narrative identity, McAdams recalls asking his students a formative question: "If you could see an identity, what would it look like? What form would it take?" He goes on to summarize the concept of narrative identity that came from attempts to answer that question:

> "We never hit upon an image that worked. But a few months later, I began playing around with the idea that identity, if you could see it, would look like a story ... When you ask people how they came to be who they are, and when you ask them to talk about the future, they typically tell stories. Imagine identity as an internalized and evolving life story, providing ... both a 'retrospective' and 'prospective' sense of a life in time, such that 'step for step, it [the story] seems to have planned him [the person as protagonist] or better, he [the person as narrator] seems to have planned [written] it [the story].'" [103]

A major implication of seeing our identity as a narrative story is that it's continuous and evolving as we go through time and history. If you will, our identity is a mystery novel whose unpredictable ending is being written *as it's being lived out*. As the main characters in our stories, we are constantly developing along with all the antagonists, advocates and supporting cast—who are also in the process of writing their own stories. Looking back, we can trace the continuity of personhood through all the "scenes" of the story of our lives. Looking forward, we are not yet who we will be when the book is closed.[104]

Our identity is a mystery novel whose unpredictable ending is being written *as it's being lived out.*

Another implication is that each of us is forming our identities as we interact with each other. Narrative identity formation is a psycho-social phenomenon, it cannot be seen as an individual process. It's inherently communal and interactive. As a result, our identity carries with it social, ethical and moral expressions. It's not just about who *I* am becoming, it's also about who *we* are becoming—together.[105]

With this backdrop, there are three things we should bear in mind as we write out the story of our identity. First, discovering identity is not something we *know*, it's something we *do*. It can't be defined and comprehended through intellect, logic and reason. Identity takes shape and gets defined through intentional, personal engagement, it must come to life. It requires active participation to walk out—or walk *toward*—your new identity, through change, trust and practice (from Part 4).

Second, we must overcome the tendency to treat our identity as fixed when it isn't. This gives our old identity a permanent and immutable status. In other words, we tend to live our lives as if the script of our identity story has already been written and we have no choice but to simply act it out as players on a stage. But this simply isn't the case. The script is being written as we live our lives ... or perhaps more accurately stated, there is no script. The process of defining our identity is more ad-lib than acting out a script.

The final point is that creating our identity is an active process, not a passive one. In other words, we can either actively shape our identity or passively allow our environment to shape it for us. If we take the passive approach (giving our environment permission to shape our identity), we lock ourselves inside an identity prison where nothing ever changes. In doing so, we submit ourselves to the impulses of the world around us. In effect, we're captives on a barge that is steered by the wind and waves of whatever environment we happen to be in at the moment.

This can be particularly damaging if our self-perception is negative, and the view we accept from others and the world is unfavorable.[106] We accept the critical, destructive self-talk from our sinful nature. We assume the lies or opinions of others are 100% accurate (despite the knowledge that those people are human and imperfect). And if our stories include significant events such as trauma or shaming, the negative self-view becomes more deeply rooted and seemingly permanent. In this prison, the only option we have is to use our old identity as the basis for who we hope to be in the future—which is as hopeless and fruitless as it sounds.[107]

In contrast, an active approach assumes our identity is being shaped and defined as we live it out. It recognizes that the prison of our past identity is real enough, but it's a prison of our own making. There are no guards forcing us to stay where we are, and the gates keeping us trapped have no locks—they would open if we merely pushed on them and walked out. But they're not going to open by themselves. We stay imprisoned for two reasons:

1. Life beyond the bars is unknown, and potentially scary.
2. We simply choose to stay where we are.

So, it all comes down to this, you don't have to be who you've always been. If you aren't satisfied with who you are, you have the choice to become the person you want to be. All you have to do is start being that person.

Simple.

Of course, simple doesn't mean easy. There is much in this world and in our broken, sinful condition that will work to keep us imprisoned. And the habits and mindsets of the old identity have been cured into place and must be actively replaced.

And of course, it also doesn't mean that a mere act of will on my part will change things that can't change or that have been damaged through some pathology. For example, I can't change my height just because I decide I want to be tall. If my leg has been amputated, no amount of intent will cause it to grow back. Remember that identity is who we are at our most basic level, at the level of self-awareness that we are unique individuals. That's where the change happens.

Being who we want to be is not easy—but it is simple. And the more we can be mindful of its simplicity, the easier it becomes.

Simple.

Which brings us to the most relevant question of all: Who is that person you want to be?

What comes to mind when you envision the person you want to be? It could be an ideal version of yourself, but since our reference point is our current identity, this is virtually impossible to envision.

Is there another person in human history you can model your identity after? I suppose you could select anyone that seems ideal to you, someone honorable, notable and exemplary—perhaps even a combination of people. And doing so would certainly point you in the right direction toward defining who you want to be.

But no matter how noble or ideal they may have been, they're still only people like you. To set up another human as an ideal identity isn't fair to them, and it misrepresents the reality that they lived with limitations, faults and shortcomings. Ultimately, this compromises the identity you're wanting to become.

As you may have already assumed, I suggest you consider Jesus Christ as the model for who you want to be. He's distinct from every other human who has walked our planet, and because of who he was—and who he wasn't—he alone is qualified to function as our ideal identity model. Let me explain why.

As I mentioned in Chapter 1, humankind (both male and female together) was created in God's image and likeness. Our nature reflected God in a way that nothing else in creation did and we were in a perfect relationship with him. Our purpose—to partner with God in managing his creation as his representatives—flowed out of our identity.[108]

This identity was lost when the first humans believed the lie that they could be like God (when they already were in every way that mattered). Their breaking off from God brought consequences, which included both the loss of their original identity and relational separation from him. From this point forward, humans have been made in *human* likeness, not *God's* likeness.[109] As a result, we now have only glimpses of what it means to embody the image of our Creator.

But then Jesus came to earth as God in the flesh. He was fully human, like us, but also fully God. That is, the identity of the second person of a triune God existed inside a shell of humanity, his "human-ness" concealing his "God-ness." But in terms of character and identity, he represented God perfectly.[110] In fact, Jesus stated that this was part of his life's purpose—to demonstrate God's identity to humanity.[111]

How would *you* respond to a homeless person who lived in obscurity for 30 years, then suddenly began claiming to be God's son?

He lived with all the human limitations we do (though without a fallen, sinful nature like us). He got tired, he had to eat and sleep. He had to learn math. He had to choose to trust God and operate his life by faith every moment of every day.

Jesus' claim of identity as God's son is remarkable, to say the least. It sounded as radical to the world in his day as it does now. After all, how would *you* respond to a homeless person who lived in obscurity for 30 years, then suddenly began claiming to be God's son?[112] Whether you believe Jesus' claim or not is a separate issue, which I'll discuss in a moment. But what's important here is that his relationship as Son is vitally significant for us, because it's similar to the original relationship we had with God before our rejection.[113]

Being identified with Jesus restores our relationship with God as his sons and daughters. Being related to him means that we have access to God again, restored to the relational status we had before mankind fell away. We acquire all the rights and privileges of a formal relationship as God's children.[114] The Bible refers to this in a variety of ways, such as being "co-heirs with Christ,"[115] "adopted children of God,"[116] and being Jesus' "brothers and sisters."[117]

You are more than you think you are. You are the only *you* that will ever exist in all of human history.

Jesus' early followers saw him as God's son—God in human form. They were eyewitnesses to his miracles and his life, death and resurrection, and they lived their lives accordingly. Having known Jesus, they never saw themselves the same way again, and their actions over the next several centuries changed the world forever.

Jesus was their model identity then, and he can be ours now. His identity is the only one capable of serving as THE ideal. It's the identity we're all searching for, the one we were created with when the world began, i.e., being the image and likeness of God.

Seizing upon this likeness means you are more than you think you are. You are the only *you* that will ever exist in all of human history. Your soul's fingerprint is unique, and God designed you to be a reflection of Jesus in your world. The challenge comes in believing this resolutely enough that you'll change from your old identity, trust in the truth and practice your new identity daily.

So, practically speaking, how do we model our identity after Jesus?

First, we have to break from our default tendency to utilize a **Backward-Reference approach** (see **Figure 1**). This approach forces us to see ourselves in light of who we were in the past, as an old identity that's corrupted, incomplete and aligned with a spiritual enemy whose purpose is to keep us blinded and imprisoned.

This approach can manifest in a couple of ways. First, we can see our identity as a fixed, permanent reality. In this mindset, it's impossible to see ourselves any differently than we always have. This is the identity prison of our own making. It needs no guards or locks on the gates to keep us in, because we're convinced we can't and won't change.

Another manifestation is a mindset that seeks identity change, but it still maintains a view of past identity as a reference point when practicing that change. It's like trying to drive forward while looking in the rearview mirror. In other words, we experiment with things in life today to be different from who we were yesterday. But because we're not clear on who we want to be, who we were yesterday is still our primary reference point for measuring that change. And all of today's experiments will be part of yesterday's identity when tomorrow comes.

Looking back is helpful for reflection. But you can't drive forward by keeping your eyes on the rearview mirror.

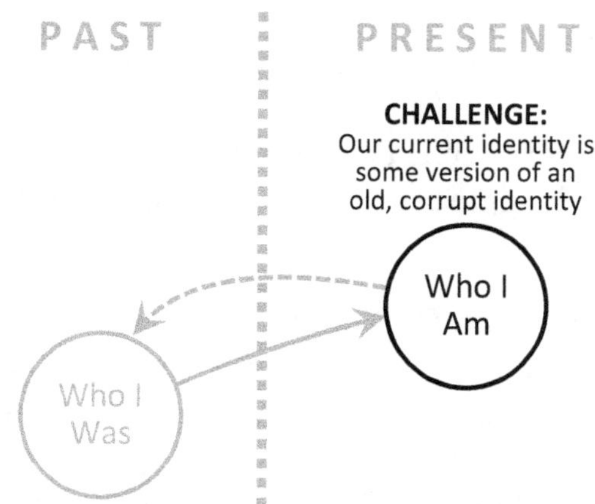

Figure 1: The Backward-Reference Approach

The Backward-Reference approach to identity creates a number of problems as we try to discover who we want to be (see **Figure 2**).

1. **Discovering a new identity is impossible.** Any concept of a new identity is a rehashed, made-over version of our old identity that, at best, we can only tweak or compensate for. Though we intuitively know there's another identity waiting to be discovered, we have no practical hope of finding it.

2. **We live experimentally.** Since we can't envision the identity we're searching for, we end up experimenting with life in an attempt to "find ourselves." We grab onto anything we believe will help define us—achievement, relationships, accumulation, status, power, gender change, career change, marriage change, etc. Continued experimenting only compounds anxiety and a troubling lack of assurance.

   This is what contributes to middle-aged adults having a mid-life crisis—a kind of desperate adjustment as they realize the available time to find themselves is starting to run out.[118] And I would argue that the more we promote experimentation, the earlier in life and more urgently the crisis appears in each successive generation. Many Millennials, for example, speak of having this crisis at "quarter-life." Gen Z's crisis is even more dramatic and is happening much earlier.

   Ultimately, experimentation is chasing after physical, temporary and finite things to define an identity that is spiritual, permanent and infinite.

3. **We default to an Outside-In approach.** This reliance upon worldly standards and identity categories is an Outside-In approach that can't confirm who we are. Things like status, achievement and preferences are not who we are, they're what we do. They are merely the caramel coating over the old identity. Even though we suspect that our outside environment is incapable of adequately defining us, we persist in our relationship with it. This creates a kind of codependent interaction with the stuff of our lives, we know it's not healthy, but we're afraid to think of who we'd be without it.

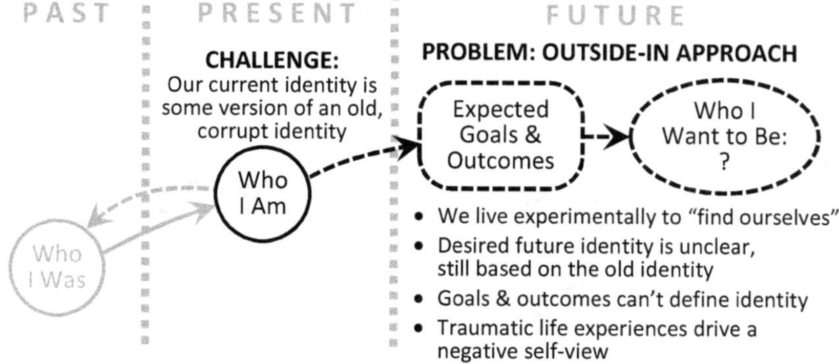

Figure 2: Applying the Backward-Reference Approach

So what's the solution?

To discover the identity we've always longed for, we must abandon all attempts at using a backward reference approach and instead use a **Forward-Reference approach** that takes us in a radically different direction than we've ever gone before (see **Figure 3**).

1. **Jesus is the model for our new identity.** Not that we can be divine, but Jesus' life, his character and values, his relationship with God and devotion to doing God's will are the restoration of humanity's original, created identity.

2. **We live purposefully.** Our purpose in life becomes straightforward, a by-product of knowing who we want to be. Instead of searching for an identity we can't define and have no hope of achieving, we apply ourselves toward living out who we know we are. The goals we set and the things we do flow out of our identity, fulfilling our deepest desires in a way that leverages our unique gifts, talents, passions and experiences.

3. **We choose an Inside-Out approach.** We no longer have to rely upon worldly criteria or achievement. The security, confidence and peace that come from knowing we are God's restored children allow us to focus on applying ourselves to make our

world better. We can work to bring God's righteousness to our surroundings by doing God's will, "on earth as it is in heaven."

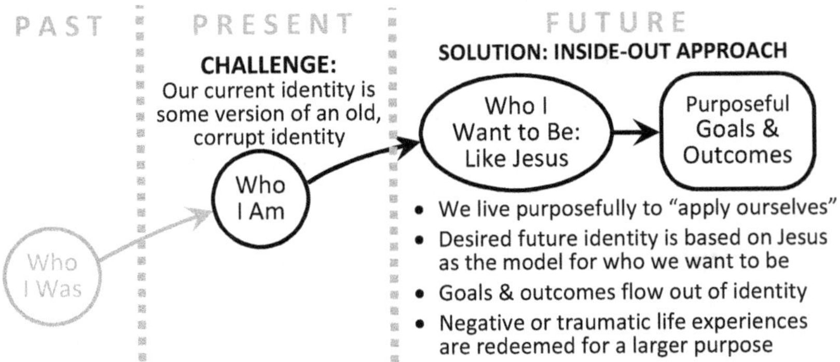

Figure 3: The Forward-Reference Approach

Discovering and living out this new Jesus-modeled identity doesn't just happen, because our default is to rely on what we've used all our lives—the externally focused, Outside-In approach that's built around our old identity. Breaking away from this approach requires taking three intentional, volitional action steps. Each of us needs to take these steps for ourselves, no one else can take them for us (see **Figure 4**).

1. **Change.** The biblical word for change is "repentance"—the act of letting go of the old identity and all its associations. It is abandoning the attempt to remake, build upon or improve the old identity and way of life. It is a complete change of identity.

2. **Trust.** Trust is belief—the act of reorienting our minds to what we understand to be true, without doubting or hedging. It often involves faith—seeing what is not visibly present or has not yet occurred, and behaving as if it *is* present and *has already* occurred. In regard to spiritual faith, it is living in this world according to what is true in God's kingdom.

3. **Practice.** Practice is described in the Bible as "obedience" (along with other words like "keep", "observe" and "follow"). It means keeping to what we trust/believe, and then living accordingly.

Continuity and consistency are what's emphasized here. It is both actively decoupling ourselves from who we were and continually coupling ourselves to our new identity.

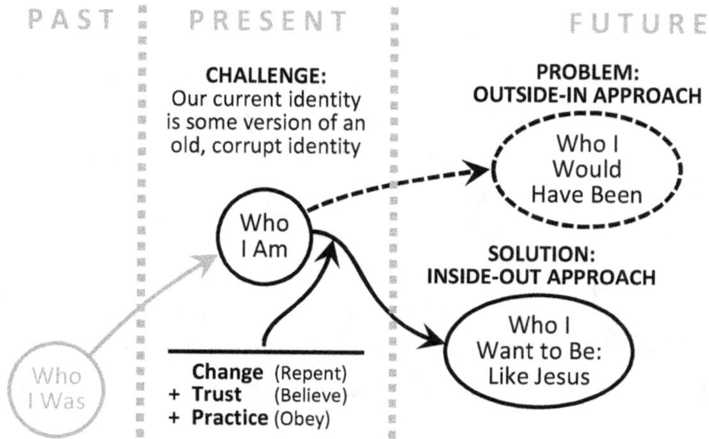

Figure 4: The Change-Trust-Practice Step

The entire process can be seen in **Figure 5**:

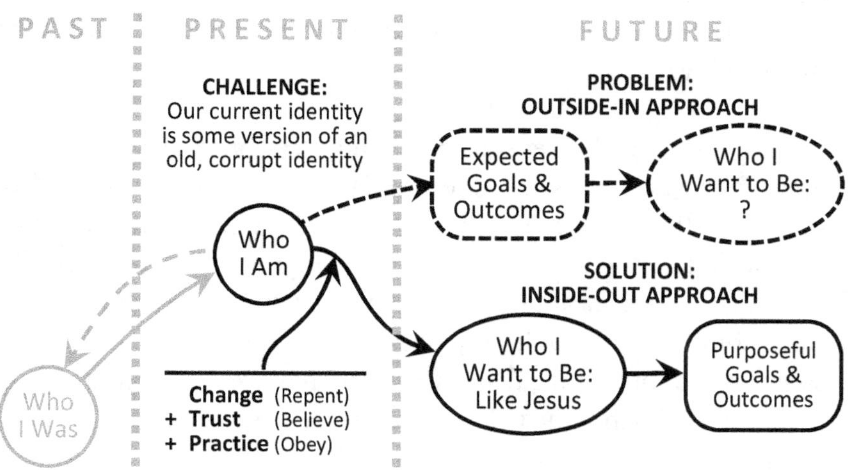

Figure 5: The Identity Transformation Process

Of course, presenting the change-trust-practice process this way might make it appear easy and clean. It is anything but. Your old identity and the beliefs, patterns, temptations and habits that went along with it do not just disappear. You will likely find that defining new ones will be challenging. Previous trauma, abuse or relational disruption you've experienced will make it difficult to trust, whether that's trusting God or trusting other people. A lifetime of believing you're who you've always been creates a lot of identity inertia to overcome. To make matters even more difficult, you face a spiritual enemy who will do everything in his power to keep you stuck in your old identity.

If you don't intentionally live according to the new identity, you will default to the old.

Living out the new identity takes discipline and effort. If you don't intentionally live according to the new identity, you will default to the old. It's as if there is a bungee cord tied to the old, dotted line of the Outside-In path you would have been on. As you begin to divert from it on the new path, a natural tension develops that pulls you back to where you were. If you're not intentional about putting change and trust into practice to live out your new identity, you will slip back into your old thought and behavior patterns and lose sight of who you want to be.

That's the bad news.

The good news, however, is that being clear on your new identity means your new habits will soon replace the old ones. As you live according to the new values and habits, the bungee cord gets stretched, so to speak, and the force resisting the change reduces dramatically. Eventually, it loses its ability to pull you off your new path.

For some of us, the pull to go back to the old identity dissolves and disappears. For others, it's always there and requires ongoing attention and diligence. Each of us will have a unique experience and story to tell regarding who we are compared to who we were.

But in any case, the solution is the same: Keep your eyes fixed on the new identity. This is about daily commitments and intentional decisions toward new behaviors as you live in the context of your new identity, while simultaneously actively rejecting the practices associated with your old identity.

Tell and retell the story of who you are and who you want to be. Make it a matter of personal meditation, then collaboration in supportive relationships (i.e., talk about it in family and community circles) that will help the identity formation process continue. Then make it a matter of celebration, because "the old has gone, the new has come."

The diagram in **Figure 5** is the "what" and the "how"—the process of knowing your true identity. But to fully understand and embrace the process, we must understand the "why" of identity—the purpose. Only then will it fully make sense.

DISAMBIGUATION
CHAPTER 15

THE BIG IDEA:

Jesus is the restoration of our lost identity.
He is the model for who we want to be.

YOU EXIST AT A SOUL LEVEL, WHERE GOD SEES AND KNOWS YOU, AND YOU ARE CONSTANTLY IN FORMATION.

Your identity is not fixed but is a narrative story being written as you go through life.[119]

DISCOVERING IDENTITY IS NOT SOMETHING WE *KNOW*, IT'S SOMETHING WE *DO*.

It doesn't happen passively, we must engage in an active process to be who we want to be.[120]

JESUS IS THE MODEL FOR WHO WE WANT TO BE.

You are the only you that will ever exist in all of human history, designed by God to be a reflection of Jesus in your world.[121]

OUR DEFAULT IS TO USE WHO WE'VE BEEN AS A REFERENCE POINT FOR WHO WE WANT TO BE.

It's helpful to look back for reflection and to understand where you came from. But it is little help for setting your sights on where you want to go.[122]

WITH JESUS AS OUR MODEL IDENTITY, WE CAN LIVE INSIDE-OUT, ON PURPOSE.

Instead of experimenting to find an identity we can't define and have no hope of achieving, we apply ourselves toward living out who we know we are. What we do flows out of who we are.[123]

WE MUST COMMIT TO ONGOING CHANGE, TRUST AND PRACTICE TO DISCOVER OUR JESUS IDENTITY.

If we don't, we'll divert back to our default reliance on the externally focused, Outside-In approach that's built around our old identity.[124]

Chapter Sixteen

Can I Get a Witness?

If God were ready to give you a new name–
and with it, a new purpose–
would you accept it?

WHEN WE ABANDON our old identity and embrace Jesus as the model for our new identity, he becomes the source of all our life's purposes and activities. Jesus referred to this as being his "disciple"—a student, a learner. What might sound like a cultic term simply means someone who adopts their instructor's teachings and philosophies, embodying them in their lives and relationships.

Considering that we want to see ourselves in light of Jesus, it's crucial that we understand how Jesus saw himself. He believed in his identity as the son of God. Jesus' identity and relationship to God the Father was the most controversial and prominent theme in his life. All his teachings and behavior were revolutionary, but his identity was the reason they crucified him. He frequently referred to himself

His identity was the reason they crucified him.

as being one with the Father, and his sole motivation was to do his Father's will. Meaning that everything he did was driven by and sourced in his identity—who he was.[125]

This identity positioned him to live a life that sometimes differed significantly from the world and its values. He wasn't trying to be radical for the sake of being a radical, he just didn't depend on the world or anything it had to offer—which gave him freedom and objectivity others didn't have. He elevated justice and mercy over rituals and legalities. He showed a propensity for using guidelines instead of rules to accommodate those who were under-served by society. He ruffled the feathers of those in power when their power got in the way of loving and caring for those who couldn't care for themselves, like the widows, the fatherless, the sick and those whom the world discards.

Jesus' identity as the son of God was his "why." He believed in it. It gave his actions meaning and purpose, making him single-minded, focused and ultimately the most influential human that ever walked the planet.

Jesus passed this same identity focus on to his followers. He taught them to abstain from the desires of their old identity, not because the desires would make them unclean but because they didn't align with their new identity. This new identity drove his followers, ultimately generating the most influential movement in human history, what one historian called "the single greatest cultural transformation the world has ever seen."[126]

We have this same opportunity today. Embracing Jesus' identity brings freedom from the enslaving passions of the old identity. It brings transformation. "Therefore if anyone is in Christ, this person is a new creation, the old things passed away, behold, new things have come."[127]

Living as this new creation looks like many of the things Jesus is historically known for, including:

- Forgiving those who've wronged us, as God has forgiven us.
- Turning the other cheek when possible.
- Giving to those in need.

- Choosing to store up treasures in heaven instead of storing up treasures on earth that will only rot and decay.
- Being kind and compassionate, not judgmental or critical.
- Being at peace, being anxious for nothing.
- Loving one another as he's loved us—without exclusion or caveat, even those who mean us harm.

Of course, we can make an effort toward these things without setting Jesus as our model identity. But that effort can only result in an Outside-In approach, where we look like Jesus on the outside but maintain our current identity on the inside. That approach may be well-intentioned, but ultimately it won't be as effective or fulfilling. Or purposeful. Who we are and what we do will not be aligned.

And if we depend on these behaviors to improve our old identity (an Outside-In, Backward Reference approach), we already know that won't work. Instead, when our identity is like Jesus' identity, these behaviors are the fruit of who we are (an Inside-Out, Forward Reference approach).

Who you choose as your ideal identity matters.

There's another aspect of embracing Jesus' identity as his disciple/follower that's important to know—it's an all-or-nothing proposal. Jesus said it better than anyone else. "Whoever wants to be my disciple must deny themselves and take up their cross and follow me. For whoever wants to save their life will lose it, but whoever loses their life for me will find it."

"Taking up your cross" referred to the public display of those condemned for crucifixion, carrying the instrument of their execution to the place where they would be crucified. It's a graphic and sobering illustration of the choice to abandon our old identity. But it's warranted, considering the seriousness of the decision.

Attempting to hold on to some part of an old and corrupted identity is actually a rejection of Jesus' identity. It's the belief that all we need is a boost from God to be who we want to be. We see him as an accessible and benevolent higher power that will complete us where we're lacking.

Refusing to surrender all of our old identity is, in effect, telling God that we don't trust him and that we prefer the control of self-determination. It compromises faith and trust, making us double-minded—part Jesus-follower and part self-follower.

Refusing to surrender all of our old identity is, in effect, telling God that we don't trust him and that we prefer the control of self-determination.

And having a split identity is not a solution.

Jesus' "take up your cross" proposal is the storage bin illustration from Chapter 6—Jesus is not something we add into the container of our life (along with everything else). Jesus *is* our life, and we gain perspective on the things we choose to add to our lives.

This is a big step to take (duh) and shouldn't be taken lightly.

On the flip side, in surrendering ourselves fully, we get the whole of his intentions for us and it's more than we ever have imagined. C.S. Lewis put it this way,

> "The more we get what we now call 'ourselves' out of the way and let Him take us over, the more truly ourselves we become. There is so much of Him that millions and millions of 'little Christs,' all different, will still be too few to express Him fully. He made them all. He invented—as an author invents a character in a novel—all the different [people] that you and I were intended to be. In that sense our real selves are all waiting for us in Him … It is when I turn to Christ, when I give myself up to His Personality, that I first begin to have a real personality of my own …
>
> But there must be a real giving up of the self. You must throw it away 'blindly' so to speak … As long as your own personality is what you are bothering about you are not going to Him at all. The very first step is to try to forget

> about the self altogether. Your real, new self … will not come as long as you are looking for it. It will come when you are looking for Him … Keep back nothing. Nothing that you have not given away will be really yours. Nothing in you that has not died will ever be raised from the dead. Look for yourself, and you will find in the long run only hatred, loneliness, despair, rage, ruin, and decay. But look for Christ, and you will find Him, and with Him, everything else thrown in."[128]

My friend Jerod said it well. "I think our culture looks at the idea of being swallowed up in submission to God as some kind of nirvana. But that's not it at all. Being in submission to God is to be forever reflecting on an endlessly beautiful God. In that place, I can finally see what isn't easy to understand—that I'm uniquely gifted. In that place, I can ask the question. What does it mean for me to be, in my space and time, the only piece of his story that he's writing through me? The world has never seen the reflection of Jesus that I am made to be."

I couldn't have said it better, so I didn't.

Why make a big deal about this all-or-nothing approach? Because you might think that assuming Jesus' identity equates to assuming the identity of Christianity as we know it. And this is not at all what I'm trying to communicate.

The history of Christendom, unfortunately, is rife with stories of people who've claimed the name of Christ and not actually trusted, changed or practiced his commands. When the church morphed from its original, relational, love-centered movement to become a social organization, it was granted political power, influence and wealth. In the Middle Ages, it eventually became corrupted and misdirected. It has since been revitalized but still retains an institutional social identity.

Currently, Christianity's public reputation is struggling—to put it lightly. Though many of Jesus' followers live quiet, faithful lives mirroring his identity, many Christians and congregations take a different approach and see themselves organizationally. Meaning that they identify themselves as a denomination, as a voting block with political platforms or as individual congregations that are unique from the congregation that meets down the street. Many (especially older) Christians identify themselves by the term Evangelical—a term that continues to lose its meaning in our society.

All of these identifiers retain elements of the church's organizational legacy from as far back as the Middle Ages.[129] When you see yourselves as an organization, you tend to identify around organizational realities—history, tradition, codes, creeds, membership, power, financial assets, buildings, popular opinion and social influence.

We see vestiges of this legacy in the prevailing model of the church as we know it, as Christianity continues to practice this organizational identity. This is not a blanket, strawman condemnation of churches or denominational organizations. Rather, it's simply a recognition that Christianity (as it's typically practiced) is a product of the culture in which it was formed and often sees itself from an organizational perspective.

But Jesus didn't give his followers an organizational identity, he gave them a *relational* identity—connecting each follower to him, to God the Father and to each other. He's asking his followers to live out this relational identity as beggars, mourners and meekers and to tell others about it. This is how he lived his life, and he asks his followers to do the same.

In his final words to his followers, he said, "... you will be my witnesses in Jerusalem, and in all Judea and Samaria, and to the ends of the earth." [130] They followed that instruction diligently, even though it brought hardship and persecution. The message of a new identity in Jesus spread throughout the Roman empire by the end of the third century. And by the fourth century, it had transformed the corrupt, paganistic culture of Rome.

Jesus didn't give his followers an organizational identity, he gave them a *relational* identity.

It was the care and concern for others—even while being despised—that won the hearts of the citizenry of Rome over to this new way of thinking. Because of the Christian values of mercy and justice, many cruel practices were discontinued or outlawed, including crucifixion, gladiatorial games, abandonment of the sick or infirmed, infanticide, and concubinage. The emancipation of slaves was encouraged, and women's rights were greatly improved.[131]

Jesus' followers in these centuries took his commands so seriously that being "witnesses" became their brand—their common, collective reputation. The Greek word for "witness" is *martyr*, a word that was transliterated into English in the Middle Ages. The word had become synonymous with their willingness to maintain their identity apart from what was happening in their environment—even in the face of extreme persecution and death.

I recognize there will be a full spectrum of reactions to the proposition that Jesus is the model for our new identity. Perhaps it feels hyper-religious, even cultic. As an American, it sounds very un-American. It might feel impractical and unproductive. Maybe it feels unrealistic or idealistic. To some, it may even sound sacrilegious.

Wherever you fall on the question of choosing Jesus as the ideal identity, I simply ask that you consider it. Don't be limited by your perception or biases of modern Christendom—whether they're positive or negative.

This is not about choosing a "religion." This is about being related to the Creator of the universe. When it comes to your identity, simply let it be a conversation between you and God. And consider that it will cost your will for your life if you do, and—potentially—your life in eternity if you don't.

Ultimately, being Jesus' disciple is the restoration of our original, created identity and relationship with God. And living out that identity by following his commands to love others[132] and to make more disciples[133] is the restoration of our original purpose (to be fruitful and multiply and manage creation). It is the ultimate redemption—the great re-purchasing and repurposing—of all the crap and sin and pain of this world. It is the fulfillment of what we will see when time is done if we believe what's written in the prophetic book of Revelation:

> "And I heard a loud voice from the throne saying, 'Look! God's dwelling place is now among the people, and he will dwell with them. They will be his people, and God himself will be with them and be their God. He will wipe every tear from their eyes. There will be no more death or mourning or crying or pain, for the old order of things has passed away.' He who was seated on the throne said, 'I am making everything new!'"[134]

Why did Jesus choose to accomplish his mission through transformed people who see their purpose as being ambassadors and witnesses? It's a fascinating question.

He could have broadcast it to the masses, to reveal himself to as many people as possible. I dare say it's what you and I would do. I have to think most marketing experts and advertising agencies would have created some kind of strategy where Jesus was the visible and evident focal point of the message, on center stage with his own website, podcast and TV channel. But when he came back to life after being crucified—a fairly marketable event—Jesus limited his exposure, appearing only to a select group who knew him and had witnessed his acts before he died. The largest of these appearances the Bible indicates was to a group of "over 500."[135]

Why limit his exposure to one of the biggest events in human history? God only knows. But I'm compelled to believe that it had something to do with the power and authenticity of a life lived out. The eyewitness testimony of someone who's lived in human form, interacted with others, influenced those they knew, followed their conscience and purposefully lived out their identity is not only impossible to deny, but it's also the most effective way to reveal the truth of God's existence.

We have to consider that it's not an accident. Perhaps God knew that the message of redemption with a new identity is more meaningful and powerful when it's told by people whose identity has been redeemed—even more powerful than proclaiming it himself.

This is evidence of the power of the story. As psychologist Dan McAdams points out in presenting the impact of human narrative identity, "It is probably no exaggeration, then, to claim that stories teach us how to be human."[136] Human and creative history is all an unfolding narrative, and we are all participants in it. Individually and collectively, the script is being written as it's being played out. We are co-creating it with God and with each other, living prose on the pages of history as our individual stories are woven together in a beautiful and terrible, tragic and epic story of loss, love and redemption.

This is your opportunity to live as Jesus lived and to love as Jesus loved. It's no coincidence that Jesus commanded his followers to "love one another, as I have loved you. By this, everyone will know that you are my disciples, if you love one another."[137] You have the opportunity to be God's extension to a broken and lost world that has never known or experienced him.

There is an unredeemed piece of his story—history—that has yet to be written according to your exact design, a narrative of redemption whose purpose is waiting to be told. No one else in the world can tell you who you should be because no one else in the world has seen it. Only God knows it, and only you can discover it. It is a one-of-a-kind discovery whose possibilities are endless. God is preparing a new name for those who follow Jesus in faith, a name carved in white stone that only he and you will know.[138]

No one else in the world can tell you who you should be because no one else in the world has seen it. Only God knows it, and only you can discover it.

It is your calling, your purpose.

Because it's your identity, who you've always wanted to be.

DISAMBIGUATION
CHAPTER 16

THE BIG IDEA:

Our true purpose is to be like Jesus and help others to be his disciples.

JESUS' FOLLOWERS ADOPTED HIS INSIDE-OUT APPROACH, AND IT CHANGED THE WORLD.

We have that same opportunity today.[139]

BEING A DISCIPLE OF JESUS IS AN ALL-IN DECISION.

We must surrender all of our old identity in order to get all the benefits of the new one.[140]

BEING A DISCIPLE OF JESUS GIVES YOU A RELATIONAL IDENTITY, NOT AN ORGANIZATIONAL ONE.

You are part of a family.[141]

JESUS CHOSE TO SAVE HUMANITY THROUGH PEOPLE WHOSE IDENTITY HAS BEEN TRANSFORMED AND WHOSE PURPOSE IS TO BE AMBASSADORS AND WITNESSES.

You have the opportunity to be God's extension to a broken and lost world that has never known or experienced him.[142]

Endnotes

Chapter One

1 Song, F. W. (2021). Restless Devices: Recovering Personhood, Presence, and Place in the Digital Age. United Kingdom: InterVarsity Press.

2 For reflection, read: Genesis 1.26-31, Ecclesiastes 2.25 and 3.19-21, Romans 8.14-17, Philippians 2.14-16, 3.1-14, Titus 3.3-8.

3 For reflection, read: Genesis 2-3, Ecclesiastes 3.11, Romans 1.19-20 and 8.18-25.

4 For reflection, read: Ecclesiastes 1-2, Luke 15.11-32, Romans 7.14-25, 2 Corinthians 4.4-6, Ephesians 2.1-2, 1 Peter 5.8-9.

5 For reflection, read: Ecclesiastes 4.9-12, Isaiah 43.1-6, Romans 8.14-17, John 1.12, 2 Corinthians 10.12.

6 For reflection, read: Ecclesiastes 7.29, Romans 8.18-30, Revelation 2.17.

Chapter Two

7 For reflection, read: John 14.27

8 For reflection, read: Romans 4.1-5, 7.21-25 and 12.1-2, Ephesians 3.16-19, James 1.5-8.

9 For reflection, read: Matthew 11.16-19 and 15.1-20, John 8.1-11, Galatians 2.16, 19-21, Philippians 3.4-11, James 1.26, 2 Peter 1.5-9.

10 For reflection, read: Matthew 7.15-27 and 23.25-28, 2 Timothy 3.1-5, James 4.1-6, Revelation 3.1-2.

11 For reflection, read: Matthew 5.23-24, Luke 11.33-36, Galatians 5.1-6 and 5.22-25, Colossians 2.16-23, James 1.26-27.

12 For reflection, read: Ecclesiastes 2.17-23, Philippians 3.7-9.

Chapter Three

13 For reflection, read: Genesis 11.4, Isaiah 53.6, Matthew 7.13-14, Luke 12.16-21.

14 For reflection, read: Proverbs 16.9, Acts 8.18-19, Romans 16.18, Philippians 3.18-19, James 4.2-3.

15 For reflection, read: Acts 24.10-16, Romans 9.1, 1 Corinthians 8.9-13, 2 Corinthians 1.12, 1 Timothy 1.5-7, 19, 1 Peter 3.13-16, Hebrews 13.18.

16 For reflection, read: Luke 12.27-31, John 15.4-5, Philippians 3.1-14.

Chapter Four

17 For reflection, read: Matthew 20.24-28, Luke 12.15-20, Philippians 2.3-4.

18 For reflection, read: Luke 14.7-11, James 2.1-9.

19 For reflection, read: James 4.13-16, 1 Pet 1.24-25.

20 For reflection, read: Matthew 6.19-21, Luke 14.12-14, 1 Timothy 6.6-10.

21 For reflection, read: Psalm 10.4, Proverbs 11.2 and 16.18-19, Romans 12.16, Galatians 6.3.

22 For reflection, read: Matthew 8.19-20, Philippians 2.5-11 and 3.17-21, 1 Peter 2.11-12.

23 For reflection, read: Matthew 5.3-5, Romans 12.3, 1 John 2.15-17.

Chapter Five

24 Hannon, Kerry, *I'm Rich and I'm Anxious*, NY Times, Nov. 7, 2017. https://www.nytimes.com/2017/11/07/your-money/wealth-anxiety-money.html

25 Ashely Lutz, Inside the Lives of America's Anxious Wealthy People, Business Insider, Nov. 8, 2017, https://www.businessinsider.com/habits-richest-people-wealthy-families-anxiety-2017-11

26 Hannon, Kerry.

27 For reflection, read: Psalm 23.1-6, Matthew 5.6, 2 Corinthians 12.6-10, Colossians 3.1-5.

28 For reflection, read: Genesis 3.1-5, Ecclesiastes 2.1-11, Luke 12.16-21.

29 For reflection, read: Psalm 10.4, Proverbs 1.1-7, 4.13 and 26.12, Ecclesiastes 10.10, Habakkuk 2:3, 2 Corinthians 10.12.

30 For reflection, read: Habakkuk 2.3, Romans 8.22-25, 2 Corinthians 4.16-18.

31 For reflection, read: Proverbs 30.8-9, Ecclesiastes 2.24-25, 5.10 and 6.7, Matthew 6.25-33, Luke 12.15, Philippians 4.11-13.

32 For reflection, read: Proverbs 11.28 and 28.22, 1 Timothy 6.6-10 and 6.17-19, James 4.1-3, James 5.1-6.

33 For reflection, read: Romans 8.18-21, 2 Corinthians 4.18, Hebrews 11.13-16.

Chapter Six

34 https://www.tampabay.com/news/courts/criminal/pretial-set-for-this-morning-in-movie-theater-shooting-case/2169793 https://www.tampabay.com/news/crime/2022/02/07/curtis-reeves-trial-all-you-need-to-know-about-the-pasco-theater-shooting/

35 https://www.nbcnewyork.com/news/national-international

36 https://www.nbcnewyork.com/news/national-international/killer-santa-lost-wife-job-dog-before-killing/1859898

37 https://www.tampabay.com/archive/2009/02/17/only-ruins-left-where-jessica-was-killed/ https://www.upi.com/topic/John_Couey/

38 For reflection, read: Genesis 6.11, Psalm 73.2-10.

39 For reflection, read: James 4.1-2.

40 For reflection, read: Ecclesiastes 1.1-18.

41 For reflection, read: John 14.27, 16.33, Ephesians 2.13-18, Colossians 1.15-20.

42 For reflection, read: Genesis 3, Isaiah 26.3, John 15.5, 2 Corinthians 12.1-10.

43 For reflection, read: Genesis 3.16, Psalm 37.4, Proverbs 16.9, Romans 6.1-10.

44 For reflection, read: Matthew 13.44-46, Luke 18.18-23, John 14.1-7 and 14.23-27, Acts 17.22-28, Galatians 2.19-21.

45 For reflection, read: Psalm 103.13-18, Matthew 6.25-34, Luke 9.23-25, Romans 12.1-2, Philippians 4.4-9.

Chapter Seven

46 For reflection, read: John 16.33, Romans 12.9-21, Colossians 3.12-17, Hebrews 12.14-15, James 3.16-18, 1 Peter 3.9-11.

47 See Ken Camp, Christian nationalism clearly evident in Capitol riot (Baptist Standard, January 7, 2021), https://www.baptiststandard.com/news/nation/christian-nationalism-clearly-evident-in-capitol-riot, and Michelle Boorstein, A horn-wearing 'shaman.' A cowboy evangelist. For some, the Capitol attack was a kind of Christian revolt (Washington Post, July 6, 2021), https://www.washingtonpost.com/religion/2021/07/06/capitol-insurrection-trump-christian-nationalism-shaman.

48 For reflection, read: Job 12.22, John 1.1-5, Acts 26.9-18, 2 Corinthians 4.6-7, Ephesians 5.8-14.

49 For reflection, read: Matthew 4.16, 5.13-16, John 8.12, 12.35-36, Philippians 2.12-16, 1 Thessalonians 5.4-11.

50 For reflection, read: Genesis 1.1-4, Isaiah 60.18-22, Luke 11.34-36, John 1.6-13, 12.35-36, 2 Corinthians 5.17-20.

51 For reflection, read: Matthew 6.22-23, Romans 2.17-29, 12.1-2, 1 John 2.3-11.

52 For reflection, read: Luke 18.9-14, Galatians 2.11-16, Colossians 2.20-23.

53 For reflection, read: Matthew 5.43-47, 1 Corinthians 13.1-3, 1 John 4.7-17.

Chapter Eight

54 For reflection, read: John 3.19-21 and 15.9-17, 1 John 2.9-11.

55 Hebrews 10.14.

56 For reflection, read: Judges 21.25, Psalm 36.1-4, 1 Timothy 1.12-13, 2 Timothy 3.1-5, Titus 1.15-16.

57 For reflection, read: Luke 16.13-15 and 18.9-14, Romans 2.1-4.

58 For reflection, read: Proverbs 30.11-12 and 16.1-3, Matthew 23.1-12, Mark 7.1-23, Revelation 3.14-18.

59 For reflection, read: Exodus 20.2-3 and 32.1-8, Psalm 135.15-18, Romans 7.15-25, Philippians 3.3-14, Colossians 2.6-23.

60 For reflection, read: Matthew 5.17-48, 2 Corinthians 3.16-18, Ephesians 2.8-9, Hebrews 10.10-14.

Chapter Nine

61 For reflection, read: Romans 1.17 and 4.1-25 Galatians 3.1-14 and 5.1-6.

62 For reflection, read: Proverbs 30.11-14, Luke 7.36-50 and 18.9-14, Romans 14.1-4, Philippians 2.3-4, James 2.1-4.

63 For reflection, read: Matthew 7.1-2, John 8.2-11, Romans 2.1, James 2.8-11.

64 For reflection, read: Matthew 7.3-5, Romans 2.3-4, James 4.11-12.

65 For reflection, read: Luke 14.7-11, Romans 12.3, 2 Corinthians 12.6-10.

66 For reflection, read: Matthew 9.9-13 and 23.23-24, Luke 6.32-36 and 15.1-7 and 15.11-31, Romans 15.1-3.

Chapter Ten

67 For reflection, read: Matthew 16.26-27, Romans 14.10-13, 1 Corinthians 4.4-5, 2 Corinthians 5.6-10, Colossians 3.23-25.

68 For reflection, read: Genesis 2-3, Ecclesiastes 7.20-22, James 3.1-12.

69 For reflection, read: Genesis 50.15-21, Proverbs 18.19, 1 Corinthians 13.4-5.

70 For reflection, read: John 8.2-11, Romans 2.1-4 and 12.17-19.

71 For reflection, read: 1 Timothy 1.12-13, Hebrews 12.14-15, James 4.1-6.

72 For reflection, read: Psalm 51.1-17, Romans 12.19-21 and 14.10-12, 2 Corinthians 5.10, 1 Peter 2.19-23.

73 For reflection, read: Mark 11.25, Romans 13.8-10, Galatians 6.1-4, Philippians 2.1-16.

74 For reflection, read: Psalm 32.1-7 and 40.11-13, John 8.36, Colossians 3.13-14, Hebrews 10.1-25.

Chapter Eleven

75 For reflection, read: Matthew 5.43-47, Luke 23.34, Ephesians 4.32, 2 Corinthians 5.16-21.

76 For reflection, read: Psalm 1.1-3, 1 Corinthians 3.1-9, Galatians 2.15-21, 5.22-23, Philippians 2.12-13.

77 For reflection, read: Genesis 1.26-31, John 15.4, Romans 12.1-3, 2 Corinthians 11.16-12.10, Philippians 3.4-11.

78 For reflection, read: Malachi 2.5-7, Matthew 7.15-20 and 12.33-37, Ephesians 5.8-10, 2 Peter 1.5-8.

79 For reflection, read: John 15.1-11, 1 Timothy 1.12-17.

80 For reflection, read: Matthew 7.21-23, Ephesians 2.8-10.

81 For reflection, read: Romans 5.1-5, Colossians 1.9-14, James 1.2-7, Hebrews 12.7-11.

Chapter Twelve

82 For reflection, read: John 15.9-17, Philippians 2.1-11, 1 John 4.13-18.

83 For reflection, read: Luke 3.1-18, John 4.4-26 and 8.3-11, 2 Timothy 2.22-26.

84 For reflection, read: Matthew 21.28-32, Luke 7.28-30, Luke 14.33, 1 Corinthians 1.10-17, Philippians 3.4-11, Revelation 3.1-3.

85 For reflection, read: Psalm 34.1-14, Matthew 16.25-26, Luke 12.15-34, Revelation 3.15-22.

86 For reflection, read:2 Corinthians 7.1 and 7.8-13, 1 John1.9, Revelation 2.1-7.

Chapter Thirteen

87 For reflection, read: Matthew 4.17 and 7.7-8, Acts 17.29-31.

88 Della Volpe, J. (n.d.). (rep.). Looking Forward with Gen Z: A Gen Z Research Report. Murmuration.

89 See Stern, C. M. (n.d.). A slow-motion crisis: Gen Z's battle against depression, addiction, hopelessness. The 74. Retrieved October 16, 2022, from https://www.the74million.org/article/a-slow-motion-crisis-gen-zs-battle-against-depression-addiction-hopelessness, and Kight, S. W. (2019, June 18). The suicide rate for 15 to 24-year-olds is the highest it's been in two decades. Axios. Retrieved October 16, 2022, from https://www.axios.com/2019/06/18/suicide-generation-z-epidemic.

90 For reflection, read: Psalm 111.10, Proverbs 1.7 and 2.1-15, Luke 21.8,

91 For reflection, read: Proverbs 14.12 and 28.26, Romans 1.18-23.

92 For reflection, read: Psalm 51.6 (ESV), 119.160, John 14.16-17 and 18.37-38.

93 For reflection, read: Proverbs 13.20, Isaiah 56.10-12, Acts 17.16-34, 2 Timothy 4.3-4.

Chapter Fourteen

94 For reflection, read: John 8.31-32, Romans 1.17, 1 Corinthians 13.4-6, Ephesians 4.15 and 5.9, Hebrews 11.1, 1 John 5.20.

95 For reflection, read: Luke 18.18-25, John 3.19-21.

96 For reflection, read: Matthew 6.25-34 and 15.1-11, Romans 4.18-21, Hebrews 11.1-16.

97 For reflection, read: Luke 7.29-30, John 6.25-40, James 1.2-8.

98 For reflection, read: Mark 4.35-41, John 14.23-24, 1 John 2.15-17.

Chapter Fifteen

99 For reflection, read: Matthew 7.24-27 and 13.44-46, Luke 6.46.

100 Atkins, Kim. "Narrative Identity, Practical Identity and Ethical Subjectivity." Continental Philosophy Review, vol 37, no. 3, 2004, pp. 341–66., https://doi.org/10.1007/s11007-004-5559-3.

101 Consider Psalm 139.1-16, Ephesians 1.4.

102 McAdams, Dan P. "The Development of a Narrative Identity." Personality Psychology: Recent Trends and Emerging Directions, edited by David M. Buss and Nancy Cantor, Springer, New York, NY, 1989, pp. 161–161.

103 McAdams, Dan P. "Narrative Identity: What Is It? What Does It Do? How Do You Measure It?" Imagination, Cognition and Personality, vol. 37, no. 3, 2018, pp. 359–372., https://doi.org/10.1177/0276236618756704. PAGE 364.

104 McAdams, "Narrative Identity: What Is It? What Does It Do? How Do You Measure It?"

105 This has been termed "emplotment": The imaginative ordering of the diverse elements of human acting and suffering into a structure that has a beginning, a middle and an end. See Atkins, "Narrative Identity, Practical Identity and Ethical Subjectivity."

106 See Atkins, "Narrative Identity, Practical Identity and Ethical Subjectivity."

107 Research shows that how we interpret events (not the events themselves) define self-perception. Meaning: If we have a negative self-identity, we tend to interpret events negatively. See McLean, Kate C., et al. "The Empirical Structure of Narrative Identity: The Initial Big Three." Journal of Personality and Social Psychology, vol. 119, no. 4, 2020, pp. 920–944., https://doi.org/10.1037/pspp0000247.

108 It's no surprise that research supports the common sense perception that a negative self-view is associated with negative well-being, such as anxiety, depression, etc. And, likewise, positive self-view is associated with positive well-being. See McLean et al. "The Empirical Structure of Narrative Identity: The Initial Big Three." PAGES 13-14.

109 For reflection, read: Genesis 1.26-27.

110 For reflection, read: Genesis 5.1-3.

111 For reflection, read: Hebrews 1.2.

112 For reflection, read: John 1.18, 14.9.

113 For reflection, read: John 10.22-39.

114 For reflection, read: Luke 3.38.

115 For reflection, read: Romans 8.14-17.

116 For reflection, read: Romans 8.17.

117 For reflection, read: Romans 8.23, Ephesians 1.5, Galatians 4.5.

118 For reflection, read: Hebrews 2.11.

119 McAdams, Dan P. "The Development of a Narrative Identity."

120 For reflection, read: Psalm 139.13-16, Ephesians 1.4-6, Philippians 3.7-14.

121 For reflection, read: Philippians 2.12-16, James 1.22-27.

122 For reflection, read: Romans 12.3-8, Ephesians 2.10, Colossians 3.8-11.

123 For reflection, read: Romans 6.1-11 and 7.4-6, Ephesians 4.17-24.

124 For reflection, read: Jeremiah 29.11-13, Romans 12.1-2.

Chapter Sixteen

125 For reflection, read: 2 Corinthians 4.16-18, Colossians 3.1-5, Hebrews 2.1 and 3.12-14.

126 For reflection, read: John 5.19, 5.30, 6.38, 10.30, 14.10.

127 Ehrman, Bart D. The Triumph of Christianity How a Forbidden Religion Swept the World. United States, Simon & Schuster, 2018, pg. 4.

128 For reflection, read: 2 Corinthians 5.17 (NASB).

129 Lewis, C. S. Mere Christianity, pp. 189–90. New York, NY: Macmillan, 1960.

130 See Gerke, Damian. In the Way: Church As We Know It Can Be a Discipleship Movement (Again), pp. 44-66. Springfield, MO: Three Clicks Publishing, 2020.

131 For reflection, read: Acts 1.8.

132 Philip Schaff, History of the Christian Church, 8 vols. (Peabody: Hendrickson, 2006), loc. 25064.

133 Commonly known as "The Great Commandment": John 13.34.

134 Commonly known as "The Great Commission": Matthew 28.19-20.

135 For reflection, read: Revelation 21.3-5.

136 For reflection, read: 1 Corinthians 15.1-11.

137 McAdams, "Narrative Identity: What Is It? What Does It Do? How Do You Measure It?"

138 For reflection, read: John 13.34.

139 For reflection, read: Revelation 2.17.

140 For reflection, read: Matthew 24.14, Luke 24.44-47, Acts 19.8-10.

141 For reflection, read: Matthew 13.44-46 and 9.16-30, Luke 14.27.

142 For reflection, read: Romans 8.12-17, 2 Corinthians 6.18.

Acknowledgments

Wow … where to begin?

Without a doubt, it takes a village to raise a book. How do you capture—in such a short list—all of the people who've invested in and shaped the formation of this book that has been captivating me for so long?

What may not be obvious is that I've been wrestling with the subject matter of *Are You Who You Want to Be* since circa 2005. An earlier version was actually on track for acceptance by a major publishing house in December 2008, but the Great Recession shut down everything in their pipeline.

So, for nearly 20 years, the longing for identity has been a topic of discussion with so many people over coffee, around the dinner table, on camping trips, and during walks on the beach. For all my friends and family who humored me and engaged in these conversations: Thank you. I'm confident that each and every one of them seasoned the thoughts in my heart and shaped the ache in my soul.

Those (relatively) early years of my writing career were, I'm sure, painful for others to collaborate with me. But in so many ways, each of them inspired and challenged me to press into the unknown of cultivating better words and prose.

I remember Dr. Robert Pyne, one of my seminary professors, took time out of his incredibly busy schedule to proof an early, horribly written manuscript for another book idea I had at the time. His edits, full of courageous truth and grace, exposed the sour, unripe fruit of my efforts. Simultaneously, they challenged and inspired me.

Thanks to Shannon and Edwin Bailey, who read so much of my stuff in the early 2000s. Shannon got her hands all dirty proofreading my stuff (see Chapter 8 for some evidence of this). Edwin's keen mind fenced with my ideas to find holes and ambiguities I didn't see. I remember on one occasion getting an essay back from him with a simple but effective edit: "No!" I got his point.

I thank Griffin, who crashed at our home for a week. His review unlocked a major reorganization of the content into largely what's in this book. Thank you, G!

I think of my sister, Dee, who's a brilliant, artful and insightful author. I still remember her proofreading (of all things) a cover letter for my first job out of college and affirmed my intent to depart from a stock approach. She read the manuscript for *Are You Who You Want to Be* and provided a timely perspective. Thank you, Sis!

Thanks to Beth Jusino, who helped edit this manuscript and challenged me on elements of writing I thought I'd mastered—but obviously hadn't. A number of times she challenged parts I thought were clear: "You need to dig deeper on this…" Your fingerprints are all over this book, and it wouldn't be what it is apart from your skillful work. Thank you for believing in me and the heart of the message I wanted to convey and giving it the clarity it needed!

Thanks to my family, Cheryl, Brennan, Ryan and Hannah—who's a skilled writer in her own right. You all have graciously accommodated me the innumerable times I've asked, "Hey, can you read this and tell me what you think?" Their observations and thoughts have all shaped the product of my writing.

Thanks to Liza Maria Garcia and the team and NOW Publishing for honoring me with their care for something so personal to me.

Much thanks to the brothers and sisters in 1Body Church, disciple-making practitioners who've inspired me with their examples of surrender to Jesus and their commitment to live and love like him.

Likewise, I'm grateful for the many practitioners I've partnered with from groups like 24:14, L1A, Biglife, NPL, Leadership Network and others. Thank you for your dedication to the mission, for your willingness to live as beggars, mourners, meekers and sojourners who are living presently and powerfully in this life even as you look forward to the heavenly life to come. Many of your stories are also reflected here in spirit, if not in literal form. It is a joy and inspiration to collaborate with you all.

Thanks go to my supporters who provided Cheryl and me the means to devote time to finishing this book (as well as my previous release, *In the Way*). Quite literally, this book could not have been produced without your offering.

The question "who am I" is part of the universal human condition. Though we were created in God's likeness, this original identity was lost. Now we're searching for an identity we've never known—with no idea what it is or how to find it. And expecting the stuff of life to define us only makes the longing for our identity increasingly desperate.

Into this desperation steps Jesus, the image of the invisible God. Being uniquely designed by God and modeling ourselves after him, we can be a custom-made reflection of Jesus in our space and time. God tells the story of Jesus through us, restoring God's original purpose for humankind in the process.

The Field Guide – A Pathfinder To Discover Your Identity And Fulfill Your True Purpose (sold separately) is written for those who are desperate to know who they really are, and who are open to discovering how God might be a part of their story—and how they might be a part of his. *The Field Guide For Are You Who Want to Be* is ideal for those who appreciate clarity and application-oriented resources. It's written as a workbook for individual or group study. It begins with the solution of a Jesus-like identity, then takes the reader through actionable and accountable steps for ongoing practice, including an annual identity-mapping process. It's available in print version with space for notes and reflection.

#AreYouWhoYouWantToBe

Resources and Connections

If the concept of being and living like Jesus did is new to you, don't worry: You are not alone, and you don't have to do it alone. There is an underground movement of people all over the world and throughout North America who are committed to follow Jesus and practicing his ways and values not as a religion, but as a way of life and an expression of their identity.

One group of people is L1A—Love One Another (LoveOneAnother.life). Go here to watch the 90-minute documentary *Love One Another Until the Whole World Knows*, which tells the story of a handful of people who are coming to understand what it means to follow Jesus. You'll also be able to find disciple-making practitioners near you, or to find more resources and training.

There is a true movement underway, one that's not led by any single brand or person. It's bigger than any one church building can contain, it's more widespread and diverse than any organization could produce. It's global, and it's local. The movement hasn't reached everywhere (yet), but it has begun. You can be a part of it, too.

Many churches, old and new, are turning toward a deliberate focus of being a disciple and helping others to do the same. There are so many groups, organizations, churches and individuals involved that it's impossible to list them all. Here is a short list of points of connection and resources:

- 1Body Church (Tampa) — 1Body.Church
- L1A (Love One Another) — LoveOneAnother.life
- No Place Left - NoPlaceLeft.net
- Underground Network — TampaUnderground.com
- KC Underground — KCUnderground.org
- Saturate — SaturateTheWorld.com
- Biglife — Big.life
- 24:14 North America — 2414NorthAmerica.net (https://2414northamerica.net/)
- 24:14 Global — 2414now.net
- New Thing — NewThing.org
- Pastor to Pioneer — PastorToPioneer.com

About the Author

Damian Gerke strives to be a beggar-mourner-meeker as he leads a life of diverse interests as an author, leadership coach, learning and development professional, church leader and disciple-making movement practitioner, husband, father and friend.

In addition to *Are You Who You Want to Be* and *The Field Guide for Are You Want to Be,* Damian is also the author of *In the Way: Church As We Know It Can Be a Discipleship Movement (Again)*. This book is written for pastors and church leaders to explain a disciple-making movement (DMM) ministry strategy. It powerfully demonstrates that the very thing we hope to accomplish—to make more disciples—is being unintentionally blocked by how we typically practice our faith, despite the best of intentions.

Damian is on the leadership team of 1Body Church, a network of simple churches in four counties in the Tampa Bay region. Simple churches are small groups of followers of Jesus who gather as peers to love God, love people and make disciples that make disciples. These simple churches meet in homes, businesses, coffee shops, gyms, prisons, parks ... wherever people gather together. 1Body has catalyzed other movements in North America and globally, and is a training hub for disciple-making movement approaches.

On the leadership coaching front, Damian has coached leaders from Fortune 500 companies to startups, in a variety of industries, and both for-profit and not-for-profit organizations. He currently partners with EntreResults, a Houston-based coaching firm. EntreResults exists to help mission-minded people create a platform to change their world. EntreResults works with businesses in the areas of strategic planning and business execution, leadership development, executive team coaching, leveraging values and culture, employee engagement and sales team training.

Damian's diverse career background has positioned him to be uniquely effective in his role as coach and spiritual leader. He has worked as a consultant and learning and development leader in a corporate HR role. He created the leadership development strategies for a company that twice made Inc. Magazine's *Fastest 5000* list as one of the 5,000 fastest-growing companies in the U.S. He has served as vocational pastor, and is a graduate of Dallas Theological Seminary. Prior to that he worked in the aerospace industry, as a structural design engineer on the B-2 Stealth Bomber project.

Damian is a Certified Professional in Talent Development (CPTD) through the Association for Talent Development, as well as an Associate Certified Coach (ACC) through the International Coaching Federation. Damian is an avid cyclist, a pastime he enjoys with his wife, Cheryl. His penchant for cycling was the inspiration for his first book *Taking the Lead: What Riding a Bike Can Teach You About Leadership*. Damian and Cheryl have three grown children. He blogs regularly about leadership and life issues at DamianGerke.com and on LinkedIn.

Go Beyond Your Leadership Status Quo

When you get leadership coaching you get breakthrough.

You may have hit a leadership ceiling, as everyone does from time to time. To overcome it, most people try harder, multitask more and work longer. But "more" (especially more of the same) won't break you through to the next level.

You need effective leadership coaching.

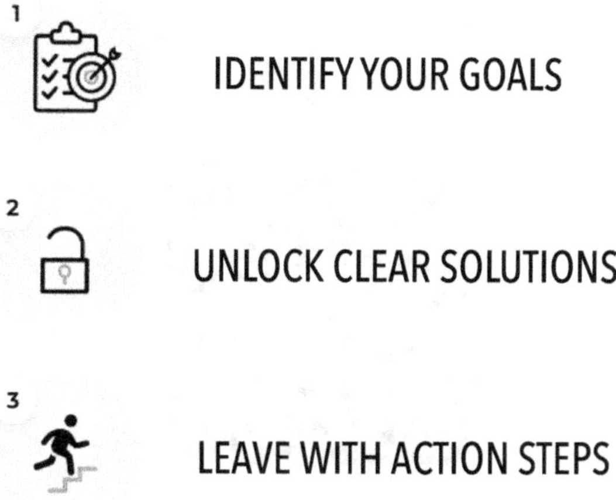

Hear from some of Damian's clients who've gone beyond their status quo:

> *"A leader must find his or her voice in order to influence and be effective. There's no 10-step program or 'app' that can ever replace or replicate Damian's approach to motivate and create results. I have found my voice. I have found purpose. But most of all, I am thankful I found Damian."*
>
> *"Damian has an amazing way of clearing the clutter from decision-making and helping you focus on the most important thing to move forward as a leader. I've been in the business world for close to 30 years and seen lots of leadership resources—his coaching is as effective as any I've ever seen before."*

Connect With Damian:

https://www.damiangerke.com/
https://www.linkedin.com/in/damiangerke/
https://www.instagram.com/damian_gerke/
https://www.youtube.com/@DamianGerke

To schedule an introductory call or book
Damian Gerke to speak to your group see QR below:

Do You Want to Make an Impact?

NOW Publishing will help you build your book and deliver your message in a powerful, impactful way.

Everyone has a story to tell and NOW Publishing is here to help them bring those stories to life. Whether you have already written a book and need a marketing partner to promote your story, or have an idea for a book that can change lives and inspire others, we are here to help you turn that into something memorable and marketable.

EMAIL US!

publish@nowscpress.com

Ask about our **90-Day Idea-to-Author** Program!

VISIT US!

www.PublishWithNOW.com

www.ingramcontent.com/pod-product-compliance
Lightning Source LLC
LaVergne TN
LVHW010607100826
845148LV00014B/2883

* 9 7 9 8 9 8 7 0 3 4 9 7 2 *